The Sexy Mama Manifesto's

Midwestern Guide to Gardening the Soul

By Jessica Dallas & Rita Stapleton

Publicity: Susan Blond, Inc

This Book Is Dedicated to

Your <u>Becoming</u>...

Table of Contents

Preface

The World Needs Women Like Us.........................…....9

Intro

Our Mission...…....13

Table of Contents

Part One: Reflections

You Are Not Doing the World Any Favors...................17

The Sexiest Woman in the World............................20

Mystery...25

Fat, Lazy, Lying Activities..................................30

The Dirty Word...44

The Quest for Faith...49

The Four-Letter Word..58

A Pocketful of Inspiration 65

Table of Contents

Part Two: 10 Steps to Gardening the Soul

0. Pre-test: What Plant Are You Overview?...............70

1. Grounding...74

2. Trimming...78

3. Reach for the Sky...89

4. Fertilizer.. ...100

5. Tending...106

6. Facing the Elements..................................114

7. Sustainable Growth..................................120

8. Beautifying Your Surroundings..................129

9. Community..132

10. Your True Plant Identity...........................139

Table of Contents

Part Three: Quick-spiration

Finding Your Joy……………………………………………....143

Beyond Competition…………………………………………....147

The Crazy Debate…………………………………………......150

Wounds……………………………………………………......153

Being Orgasmic Without Assistance………………………....159

Prescribing the Cause……………………………………….....162

Influence V. Dominance……………………………………...167

The Elevator Speech…………………………………………....173

Vulnerability…………………………………………………179

The Psychic Makeover…………………………………….....183

Table of Contents

Part Four: Meditations

Recommitting & Focusing Daily..............................189

Anger..191

Neutrality..194

About Us..199

Coming Home...206

Table of Contents

Appendix

Glossary...208

Relaxation Script...212

What Type of Plant Are You Quiz.............................217

Plant Index...227

The World Needs Women Like Us — And Like You

We love you, ladies.

We love you and we don't even know you, per se.

We love you because we feel a sense of kinship to all ladies of the flyover states.

We believe there is a sense of honor and dignity that is shared amongst us and that gives us the potential to be the sexiest mamas on the planet.

We love you because we are just like you- and, we know some of you don't know how to love yourselves.
So you need our support. Our help. Our encouragement.

We love "flyover" gals because, like you, the two of us have gone through some *stuff* with varying degrees of success and have come out on the other side.

The main difference between you and us, at present, is our level of happiness.

We are two ridiculously happy chicks. We are ridiculously happy because we are wickedly intelligent, sexy and inspired. Much like you can be.

We would like to take the opportunity to relay our inspiration to you in the hopes of perpetuating more of our kind because the world as we know it only benefits from community- and quite frankly is in dire need of some fabulously inspired women.

So many women in the Midwest approach us and ask us how we did it. How we managed to become creatures of our own design and ambition. They see our worldly accomplishments and attribute it to luck or fate. That attitude- that it was predestined- is entirely counter productive because it does not account for US- and it does not account for YOU.

We're here to tell you that our success had more to do with our concerted effort. And the good news is this success can be easily remanufactured if you apply it as we have. You just have to be willing and give up the idea that the stars are conspiring against you. It is an idea that both of us had to give up on, and once we did, our lives began to take on a course of happiness, peace, joy and sexiness that is continuing to grow to this day.

We are here to show you ladies that the universe rights itself if you align your soul with your G-D and your GGTs (Grace Given Talents) and you are willing to put all of your focus, energy and your belief systems into finding and growing your authentic self.

How do you find her? Well, dah-leengs, authenticity and Sexy Mama status doesn't come over night, nor does it come without making some serious changes on your part. But if you are committed to following the 10 steps we have identified in this book, we promise you that at the end of the journey you will emerge with a new method of thinking, being, and a new authentic "you" that will be *unstoppably sexy*.

What is a sexy mama?

We use this term as our "tongue in cheek" celebration of every woman's potential…

Especially the women of the flyover states who have been largely overlooked by mainstream media.

You ladies have been barraged with images of what the west and east coasts consider sexy, ie: physical perfection, acquisitions, and power - but this doesn't necessarily reflect what *her* ideal of sexy is… Which leans perhaps toward the internal, the spiritual… A balanced beauty… A contentment

Quite simply: **a sexy mama is a woman of any age and stage who is happy on her own damned terms**.

We are passionate about helping our flyover gals become sexy mamas and this book is dedicated to helping you through that process.

So…

Of all the life events, choices and situations we counsel women on, overwhelmingly the most immediate matter that women want to discuss and get resolved is how they relate to men.

So we think we'll strike the most gold across the board by using this topic as the primary introduction to the material you are about to receive. And here's some more good news- this same perspective can be applied to every area of your life. That is of course if you are willing. If you let it.

In the true spirit of self-help, we're going against the competitive mindset in order to give you some short-cuts for getting the man you want. This is something we wish our female forbears had relayed to us. So many of them simply didn't have the man they WANTED-but rather- the man they got.

And the life they got. And the career they got. And the body they got, etc...

So we're going to inspire you out of that rut. We are going to give you a good dose of it.

If you put these words into effect in your life you will evolve in marvelous ways. You will be unable to hold yourself back. You will be unable to keep yourself from inspiring the women around you in the course of your daily activities.

The flyover revolution of sexy mamas will begin!

And like we said- the world could use some more fabulously inspired women.

Some Real Sexy Mamas.

Our Mission

We are going to give you a spiritual answer to your relationship, career, emotional and other problems.

We're assuming you have them if you are reading our book.

We feel uniquely qualified to discuss these issues because we were just like you. We were Discontented American Women (DAW's) living in the Midwest, as they will be known hereafter.

We started out poor, stupid and childless so we had sense enough to go to college to get degrees. Kind of the natural order, eh? Those degrees brought eventual careers and those careers went on to provide for our eventual children.

And yet we were discontented still.

We thought if we got a pleasant man who didn't have any visibly disgusting habits then we'd make pleasant babies with him. So we found the man, had the babies, juggled our careers, and tried to keep our individual identities.

And yet we were discontented still.

We had the so-called perfect house, perfect car; our kids went to perfect schools. It was all very Stepford, in retrospect. Sure we had awareness of bigger systemic problems like poverty and lack of access to healthcare for the majority of the world but we were way too busy bemoaning our own issues.

Our thighs were fat.
Our kids were disrespectful.
Our clothes weren't chic enough.

Our outsides, as DAWs, were more important than our insides.

We should have been waking up every morning, thanking the Divine Energy of the Universe for the fact that we were living in a free society, had access to education, healthcare, and a means of improving our circumstances.

But we weren't.

We were being whiney little bitches.

Because as DAWS, **our outsides were more important than our insides**.

In all of the outward striving toward acquisition, love had become just another thing to "get."

Love was supposed to be a natural byproduct of increasing wealth and success.

In retrospect, it was just the opposite.

Love is not something to be attained. Love is a state of being.

Looking back, we can say that we were discontented because we didn't know what love was.

We were discontented because we were not being true to our authentic selves. We hadn't done the work required to be real authentic beings. We were sleepwalking through our lives and forgoing responsibility.

We've got news for you ladies. There is no Capricious Higher Power sitting upstairs arbitrarily assigning a more beautiful fate to the predestined great among us.

There are no Sacred Muses whispering inspirations in others' ears over your own.

Society is not screwing you.

Motherhood is not stripping away your free time.

It's not your ignorant husband or your selfish boss who's sucking your life's blood from you.

You are responsible for your own life.

You are responsible for your own happiness.

You make decisions and you have resources.

And if you happen to be living a life you don't approve of perhaps it is because you've insisted on believing the truth of others over your own. We're here to encourage you to rewrite that storyline. We're here to encourage you to move toward your own actualization.

Because when you are actualized you are by far, the sexiest, most compelling thing on the planet. Do you hear that? A self-actualized woman is a fearless woman and a fearless woman is one sexy mama!

The perfect circumstances fall naturally into place. Opportunities arise that you never thought possible.

And that hot ass partner that you spent your life chasing is just the icing on the proverbial cake.

So, hang on ladies. Whiners beware! We will challenge you, we will push you, we will make you question yourselves and, at the end of the journey, you will abandon your DAW status and *unleash the sexy mama* within.

This is our promise to you.

You Are Not Doing The World Any Favors By Being An Idiot

The world has enough of them already. Let's not provide the rest of the world the ammunition they need to support their notions that Midwestern and Flyover women are overweight, uneducated, unmotivated and un-chic.

You're also not doing the next woman any favors by perpetuating idiotic encounters with ignoramuses who you're convinced deserve a psychic makeover that only YOU can provide.

Your talents, little lady, lie elsewhere. Trust us on this.

You are not responsible to remake the goods upon delivery, be they animal, vegetable or mineral. The goods should suffice when the order was originally placed. If not, please promptly return the merchandise.

With all of the men available in the world, why are we as women so intent on behaving like idiots and hanging onto a specimen who isn't suitable for us? A breathing male is not a "quality" ladies.

Set your sites higher. Midwestern women are smarter than this.

You are not the host of "Extreme Boyfriend Makeover".

If you know your authentic self, you can be honest with about any dude you allow into your world. You need to tend to yourself first and know what type of woman you really are!

Newsflash: It's up to us, as women, to define what we need. When we know what we need we can effectively communicate those needs to our potential mates up front. In doing so, we reduce the amount of energy spent kissing frogs. We're focused on improving ourselves and getting the damn prince we deserve.

We like to use the metaphor of gardening for the spiritual tending that we are encouraging you to do.

In the flyover states, we know all to well that in gardening there are certain eventualities.

There will be sun.

There will be clouds.

There will be rain.

There will be droughts.

And if you cease growing you will be mistaken for food.

How you respond to these conditions, dear lady determines what kind of life sprouts around you.

We like to think of every woman in flowering terms. It's probably the Georgia O'Keefe in us. For those of you who are new to gardening, and lack a green thumb, have no fear. Each plant is unique, each is a little funny, and each has characteristic beauty and resilience. Each one kicks buttinski when it knows what it is.

We want you to know who you are and go out and celebrate it.

Cuz when you know who you are you infuse yourself with power.

Sexy Mamas Of the Midwest   18
Dallas - Stapleton
Guide To Gardening Your Soul

You are being honest.

And when you know who you are you can state up front to anyone and anything what you want.

You stop fearing the rain, the drought, and the parasites. You start to live on light and light alone.

But before we get too esoteric, let's get back to our gardening fundamentals.

If it's acceptable to be in a relationship where you're not nurtured then you might be Ms. Holly.

If it's acceptable for you to nurture others before yourself then you might be Miss Buttercup.

If you require the attentions and affections of others at all times then you might be Madame Rose.

We'll get to know all of the Plant Girls as we go, but suffice it to say upon completing our book and identifying your plant totem it is your responsibility to present that reality to the outside world.

And if your dream dude doesn't respect and enhance the plant that is YOU then you need to tell him to find another field to plow.

> **Helpful Hint:** When you state your needs up front with your partner then the relationship is between two consenting adults. It's like employment at will. Either one can leave at any time. This is not the age of arranged marriages and making the best of what you have. This is the age of honesty and endeavor. So go get it, girl.

The Sexiest Woman in the World

In the spirit of keeping things honest, we the experts, are just going to spell it out for you.

Men, whether from East, West or Midwest want good lays and short conversations. At some point, if things get serious, perhaps they'll contemplate your ability to beget their unborn children, but for most part, they're not there yet. Sadly enough, most men want the hot, low maintenance chick. Deal with it.

The good news is, women from the Flyover states, due to lifestyle, commitments to faith, family and friends tend to meet the low maintenance criteria more than other women.
  Newsflash: Men are hunters NOT gatherers. They are task oriented

The way they select a mate is the same way they select anything. Hunt it, gather it.

If a man wants a plant for his home, he will go to a store that specializes in plants to get one.

He is going to buy the prettiest, heartiest plant he can find, and the one that appeals to his eye the moment he sees it.

He will not spend hours laboring over whether to buy one particular plant over another smaller, less pretty plant. He will not spend valuable time attributing "good qualities" to the crumpled up pathetic looking plant that perhaps needs some good fertilizer.

A man will not call his best friend from the store to get advice on which plant to select. His choice will be the most vigorous, heartiest plant that he knows will require the least amount of tending.

> **Man:** Man need plant, uga, uga!!

> **Plant 1:** Pick me, pick me. Hey big boy, over here! Look, I'm the pretty plant!

> **Plant 2:** Look at her, throwing herself at that man. Well, if he doesn't see how perfect I am even though I need a good pruning, then screw him.

> **Plant 3:** I just hope he notices me. I look like all the other plants here…. Sigh…

> **Man:** Ahhhh… this perfect, pretty, hearty plant is the one.

A man wants to bring the plant home and move on with his daily life. He will not lament about where to put his new plant. He will not redecorate for the plant. He will not move his favorite lazy boy chair to make room for the lovely new plant.

He certainly will not put up special plant lights to encourage her new growth. He will not purchase fertilizer. In fact, the man will put his plant exactly where he finds an empty place.

It is possible the man may decide to have all of his friends over to watch the game and not even acknowledge or introduce his new plant to them. He likes his life just the way it is. Shouldn't the plant?

> **Plant:** Hello? Umm… You don't expect me to sit on THAT shelf do you?

Man: Uga, uga!

Plant: The lighting in here is all wrong for me; you should go to the Tool and More store and fix it for me. Oh, and while you're at it, how about a nice doily to put me on?

Man: Uga, uga… What's a doily??

Do not be surprised if the man goes about his daily life and routine and suddenly forgets to water his plant. It may sit on the shelf for days, possibly weeks without any attention or nourishment. Does this mean he doesn't love his plant? No! It *means he is interested in other things outside of botany.* This is a good thing. It means he is a fully developed human being with his own sense of identity that was present before he got the plant, before he moved the plant in and will continue to be there whether or not the plant withers and dies or in fact lives.

Plant: Hello?? I need attention. You haven't talked to me in days and all you do is hang out with those smelly friends of yours. When are you going to spend some time with me? Just the two of us?

Man: Uga, uga? I thought you were fine. Hey now, if you don't like it, I can always go get a new plant!

Plant: (plant exhales loudly and dirt splatters all over his plasma screen TV)

Perhaps you find this "plant-ist" or discriminatory against all plant-kind.

Newsflash: Men don't personalize. They are not nurturers in the classical sense. And if you're a red-blooded American female, that's why you love them.

Men are encouraged to develop their identity from the time they are born. Women chase men who are in pursuit of their dreams as if self-identity is something they can parasitically absorb within the context of a relationship. This sort of foreclosed upon existence traps us as women in perpetual childhood, under the continual influence of the more mature individuals, often the men in our lives. So what happens to us when that relationship ends? We gain twenty pounds, go back to therapy, then visit a plastic surgeon to get the new twenty taken off. We spend our hard earned money on products to "fix us" and lament our cruel fate while the man in question simply moves onto the next willing participant.

You do not need to continue on in this fashion, ad infinitum, until some sort of Benevolent Fate steps in and rewards you with your knight in shining armor!

You can save yourself.

You are perfectly capable.

Men have enough to do in the realization of their own hopes and dreams. Don't rely upon them to bring yours to fruition. Don't wait for a man to save you from a cruel and twisted future.

Flyover women were raised to be stronger than that. We weren't given silver spoons, expense accounts, and put on pedastools that we didn't earn.

We had after school jobs, we worked in the family businesses, we helped our single-mothers, we got involved in our schools and communities, we valued our girlfriends, we were raised with strong faiths and we were told we had to earn our educations and being "pretty" wasn't going to cut it.

Remember your roots ladies. If you were raised in the Flyover states, chances are you can change the tire on your own car, possibly milk a cow, drive in the snow, plant a garden without killing something, play backyard football, have a few skinned knees and know what it's like to sit for hours on cold bleachers in the rain to root for our favorite team. We're survivors!

So, it is our fervent hope, ladies that we might all get fired up about something that isn't the human male.

Don't get us wrong. We are not advocating a battery powered and vibrational existence courtesy of Doc Johnson. Men are delicious and deserving of our company but this must be on our terms as well as theirs.

Relationships, in their highest incarnations are partnerships between two self-actualized human beings. They are NOT opportunities for the lazy and desperate among us who wish to skip out of defining and achieving what is clearly within their grasp (self actualization) in order to fulfill some sort of socially contrived role.

So men get a leg-up on us, socially speaking, in how they are encouraged toward independence and autonomy. So what? We, as women, have done enough crying over spilled milk. Be brave enough to realize your own vision of self.

And if you haven't the bravery within you, at this moment… Borrow some of ours…

A Self actualized woman is the sexiest woman in the world!

Mystery

Most women come to us when they're leaving a relationship. It's a shame that they seek us out when they're feeling broken and unhappy and are willing to pay a professional to tell them what's wrong with them.

So we do. And more often than not it has everything to do with defining what is sexy and what is not.

And more often than not, the number one piece of dating advice we give women is to **talk less.**

Newsflash: Femininity to most men equates with mystery. You are not mysterious when he can tell your entire family history from birth to present. Save that for later, when a long term relationship is built or possibly not ever. You don't have to filet yourself for someone else's benefit. Allow yourself the dignity you deserve.

For all you exceedingly intelligent women out there- don't take the pitfall we did. Don't give your dude more emotional credit than he deserves. Quite frankly, my dears, men just aren't as abstract as we think they are. We may think that they are following our ramblings of yesteryear but they are not. They're usually reflecting upon the game on the TV in front of them.

Most men live in the present. You rarely hear a man blaming his current failures on the pony he didn't get as a kid. Some women love to live on memory lane. They park their groove-thangs there so frequently that there are permanent bun-marks in the pavement.

Instead of lamenting the past and sharing each tribulation with your new partner, how about keeping some of that effed up sha-bang to yourself and letting him see the current, powerful you? Does he need to know all that you went through to get you to the spot you are at today? Not at all!

In fact, darlings, men find the past exhausting because it suggests that he has to go out there and do battle with yet another saber tooth tiger, which is, in your case, your effed up past. Men are concrete, black and white, and all the psychedelic colors of your past will not dazzle him but distract and exhaust him.

Men like gray. Other colors confuse him.

If you confuse and exhaust a man, he will not want to have a relationship with you because he can find dozens of women who are prettier, hotter and younger without listening to their "issues."

Why do men love younger, less intelligent women? Because they think nothing, say nothing and share nothing. They are blank canvases to project the male fantasy upon. They are *uncarved blocks* in the Buddhist sense. They're the ultimate studio audience for the average male!

And now... A word to our competitors, the whores, who are out writing lots of books too.

Ahem...

Whores are the antithesis of the mysterious woman and nothing you need to bother with. A cousin of our friend, the Younger, Less Intelligent Woman, a Whore can be any age, make or model (literally). Hopefully you've spent some time in Whoreville and have figured this out on your own, but for those of you who haven't here's a brief overview...

Whores are the ultimate to the average male. They're attached to nothing and no one. They have no identity of their own. There's no Whores Union looking out for their interests. They have no institutional power so it's not like there are any consequences for screwing them over. They appreciate the male gaze, however momentary, and are prepared for their inevitable moving on when it does occur. A man never commits to a Whore so he never has to worry about marrying one.

To the average male a Whore is fantastic. She's the ultimate fan club. There are no expectations. Perhaps she's barely of-age. Perhaps she's a well seasoned executive assistant. The point is she knows nothing so she demands nothing. She pours on the porn star sex. She has no self-respect: she's just an orifice.

A lot of women call themselves feminists but what they really are Whores with College Degrees and we mean that in the most *loving* sense.

Jessica can speak a bit about this because she spent some time in Whoreville. Jessica was a Whore Feminist who dressed up her troubles with intimacy in a provocative laissez faire sexual extravaganza for about 10 years until she exhausted herself. In the midst of a rather profound bout of chronic fatigue, Jess realized how counterproductive such Whoreville residence was toward the realization of long term fulfillment and happiness.

Interestingly, she spent this time in Whoreville, when she abandoned the Midwest for the East coast and lived in the Big Apple. She took a huge bite of that city and fell into the trap of living the "life" and forgetting her roots, where she came from, and what "home" and the comforts of the Midwest provided her.

Yes, she loved sex but she sure as hell didn't love the Sabine aftermath. Then the adventure commenced, for dear ol' Jess… But we'll get to that later…

Happiness and peace take work once you've encountered the realization that *life is often unfair and that we aren't the princesses we thought we were when we were three...* That there's always someone more beautiful, intelligent, and charismatic waiting around the bend. That we will grow old, grow less sharp as we age, and become increasingly burdened with real world responsibilities. *But you know what, lovelies? That is a-okay.*

Because absolutely everything is unfolding perfectly.

A big ole nasty case of frustration and exhaustion is a great justification to start the deep dive inward.

And the Deep Dive, as we call it, is the stuff that comprises our 10 Steps to Gardening the Soul and helps to uncover that fundamental question to every woman:

What is the stuff that makes me worth loving?

You are unique, dearest. You know that, don't you? If you don't, you are about to learn it.

You are <u>so much</u> bigger than the sum of your parts (tits, teeth, hair, legs, hoo-ha).

And the thing with Whores is this- they don't realize how wonderful they are. Jessica sure didn't. She sold herself short. She rushed into sex thinking that the beast with two backs would offer salvation from the internal strife and riot of not knowing her true nature, which was so loved.

We know plenty of Glamazon Whores who've married into lifestyles and were purchased by men just like your average streetwalker on the corner...

However, we'd wager that your average prostitute is a bit more honest. At least she didn't have to live with her "John" or have little Johns or Johnettes with him.

So here's the big **Ahem**, or point, as we are coming to it…

Beauty doesn't last, darlings. Even the most gorgeous Russian nymphette, fresh off the boat, with the most delicious parts according to male standards, *will age at some point.*

Eventually somebody's not going to want to stick it to even the hottest piece around, including the residents of Whoreville.

So do yourself a favor and stop cloaking your true Grace Given Talents (GGTs) with an overwhelming focus on your external qualities and get interested in your uniqueness because that 16" waist isn't going to last forever.

Besides, dark nights of the soul are so much easier to clean up when we're not old and infirm.

Fat, Lazy, Lying Activities

You start out as this perfect, clean little thing. A pretty little newborn. Bright-eyed and expectant. A whole world of possibilities…
Baby: Goo goo! Ga ga!

We all recognize that babies are very much shaped by their circumstances. After all, they are just little things.

Mom: Here you go baby, a nice big bottle…

Baby: Mmmmmm… [*baby drinks from the bottle and promptly barfs.*]

Here's the deal, though… For everyone, even babies… Life happens to us all no matter what. Circumstances occur. The proverbial fecal matter hits the fan.

And being fragile little things we almost always adopt the traditions of our biological tribe (our family) as a means of surviving the unpredictability of life.

And if your mom liked to stuff you full of formula as a kid, you will probably stuff yourself as an adult.

If your dad liked to make you *work* for his attentions, then you will most likely do the same dance as a woman with the influential men in your life.

However…. The world that we live in views us in terms of our ability to <u>keep living</u> and thriving regardless of the opinions and oppressions expressed by our families of origin.

The world is, in fact, tremendously resilient and spiritual. You don't need to be an environmentalist to pick up on that fact.

And of increasing interest to us is the fact that the institutional world as constructed by men doesn't give a fig about your details dah-leeng. Read up on your world history, if you doubt us. Most of the world was built and operationalized by men, remember, and men are not detail oriented. They are hunters NOT gatherers, remember?

In other words, the world doesn't give a toot how we started out cute and ended up with a huge buttinski.

The world could care less how we were once so soft innocent and now you're a rigid little anorexic malcontent.

The world views you in terms of your **external** features at first glance.

Your loved ones will view you in terms of your **internal** structure.

If the external or internal is out of whack your life will become increasingly difficult.

In short, you need to be hot AND sane on your own terms in order to thrive in this deal we call life.

And whether or not you're an obvious freak in the beginning (fat), an emerging freak two months into the relationship (lazy) or a discontented freak after the kids head to college (lying), the point is you will be unfulfilled and unhappy because you are engaging in fat, lying and lazy activities.

Fat, lazy, lying activities are the spiritual vampires of the sexy mama.

Fat, lazy, lying activities are the leeches of positive self regard.

Here's why…

If you look like a person who has not taken care of your physical body, others will assume that you are engaging in fat activities.

If you look like a person who has skated by on her laurels as a kid but not done much in terms of progressing as an adult, the world will assume that you are engaging in lazy activities.

If you look like a person who is pretty and fit but has to parade around in spandex to prove her worth, the world will assume that you are engaging in lying activities, because *who honestly feels comfortable in spandex?*

Men don't want to be with fat, lazy, lying women. Nor do many self-empowered sexy mamas- the women who will make the best friends you'll ever come across.

We are here to save you from perpetuating the belief that you can continue to do fat, lazy and lying activities and still lead a healthy, happy and productive life in this world.

Here's the thing with fat, lazy, lying activities. Unless you are a complete sociopath lacking insight (a clinical anomaly in psychological terms), you have a moral compass and *you know when you're engaging in the FLL's.*

That's where your self esteem comes from- identifying with your personal strength to rise above your immediate emotional need to eat the cheesecake or sit on the couch or misrepresent your accomplishments to a seated audience.

There is no peace if you're fat. The world judges you, you internalize their judgment. There's no peace if you're lazy. The world judges you, you internalize their judgment. There's no peace if you're a liar. The world judges you, you internalize their judgment.

It's a freakin' fact.

But if you think you're going to be the first fat, lazy liar with high self esteem then by Jehosefat, go ahead, have at it. Let us know what you figure out. We may be wrong. We ourselves have tried to make it happen and in the end have come to believe that the fastest path to peace is to stay busy, stay honest and stay fit in body, mind and spirit. Our Midwestern values taught us this. Fat, Lazy and Lying activities didn't advance our communities, they didn't help our schools, raise our children or create good, decent families.

The Fat

Fat activities are categorized as anything you are doing that keeps your body, mind and soul "fat".

Take some time right now to look through your day and think about things activities you are doing that could help you get rid of those extra pounds. Stop doing Fat Activities today!

Rita has 4 kids at home and finding time to go to a regular gym is not always easy, in fact, she hates it, so perhaps you can take some hints from her. Simple choices you can make today will help and will start eliminating Fat activities.

Rita does her "push ups" as she gives her daughter a bath and plays "peak-a boo"
She has a rule with the stairs and elevators: Elevator only if up more than 2 and down more than 3
She does her sit-ups or mild weights during her favorite TV show
She tries to eliminate Fast Food and packs healthy snacks for her desk
She parks as far from the entrance as possible (make sure it is a safe spot)
She has a rule in her house "no eating in front of the tv". This encourages hungry eating rather than binge or boredom eating (including the children)

She doesn't drinking any high-calorie drinks or sodas
She gets exercise by carrying loads of laundry up flights of stairs
She "dances" with her kids while she cleans the house and makes sure
she bends up and down a lot
She doesn't try to carry all of her groceries in at once to encourage
multiple trips and therefore a lot of walking

Women who are successful at keeping their bodies, minds and souls
"Fat free" have learned to look for sources of inspiration other than
food. They choose to walk their dogs, carry their children, cook
healthy meals at home, and move, move move.

If we don't move our bodies it will age faster. The older we get, the
worse it will become. There is nothing sadder to us than to see young
girls who have already lost their shapes and haven't even "lived" or
gone through child birth. We have had 6 pregnancies between us and
lost all our pregnancy weight and never looked better. We attribute
this to that we haven't adopted fat activities.
Growing up in the Midwest and having access from a young age to
healthy, Ohio grown veggies gave us both a jump start on how we stay
fit.

Rita's mom had traditional values and stayed home to raise the
children. She was raised on a huge garden of fresh vegetables that
were later canned and frozen for the winter, fresh baked goods and
home cooked meals every day. Her lunches were packed and she
didn't know about "store bought" cookies and cupcakes until much
later in life. Adopting this "fresh" approach to eating contributes to an
"Non-Fat" lifestyle that taught her body to reject the "Styrofoam" in
store bought goods and only a Midwest lifestyle can provide.

We recommend looking through your life and find a fat activity to
remove each week.

Additionally, taking onus with Fat Activities is not about disowning the curves and beauty of the feminine form.

This is about getting closer to the form our spiritual selves would have us embody in an effort to serve others with less interference and fatigue from our physical selves. Our Midwestern/Flyover values taught us to respect our spiritual selves and physical forms.

The process of letting go of Fat Activities will bring up the Ugh Voice as we call her, the under-evolved part of you that is still afraid of the dark and whose existence feels threatened as you begin to get more authentic. Why? Because she will no longer be running the show!

In reducing your intake of Fat Activities your Ugh Voice will begin to scream and as she begins to rip you a new one, thank her extra pounds of pain and layers of emotional blockage that kept you safe from whatever reality was way too much to face at the time.

We are here to tell you though, darling girls, that the days of the Ugh Voice running the show are numbered. You are so ready to face the dark. You are so much bigger now. You have means, you have agency, and you have LOVE. If you follow the suggestions in this book, you will have access to an emotional and spiritual center that you weren't even close to possessing back in the day. You are moving toward full integration of mind, body and spirit, which is the destiny of the Sexy Mama.

So go on, now, get your physical self in gear. Now is the time to develop the strength and fortitude for living. However that plays out in your body is your business.

Helpful Hint: Reduce your consumption of processed and less nutritious foods and increase your consumption of fruit and vegetables. If you can, buy organic produce. Organic fruits and veggies have more vitamins and minerals in them, requiring you to eat less to be "full." Most of the time we have the urge to "graze" because our bodies are starved from nutritive elements and minerals. Go get yourself a kick-ass supplement like spirulina, dah-leeng, and start noticing how much better you feel!

The Lazy

Lazy is just another word for selfish. Selfish, self-absorbed women don't get very far.

These are the chicks who're caught up in their own creation myth, the chicks who've stopped growing, and the chicks who are about as dynamic as our left feet collectively.

These chicks have a million and one reasons why they've got it goin' on. Maybe they're not quite as externally effed up as the Fat Actors above, but if you get yourself around a lazy woman, watch out. It's infectious.

Lazy females are the ones who sit on bar stools talking about the Vogue Magazine they were in 6 years ago. Lazy females are the types who marry well in order to hurry up with the relaxation. What a bunch of bunk. Now come on now, ladies, when did lethargy do anybody (especially women) any freakin' good?

Lethargy is a poison. Lethargy uses depression to get down in your guts and convince you that you are powerless. Powerlessness is a learned condition. You didn't come out of the box believing that. Powerlessness is something you fed through inactivity. It's a complete waste of time.

We are not powerless! As we said in earlier chapters, we Flyover Gals know how to operate power tools, change tires, drive standard shift cars, works several jobs at a time if necessary, raise our children without a man and bring home to bacon on the side. We don't need to lie in bed and wallow in self pity and wait for the next "big thing" to rescue us because we are too busy shoveling our driveways, running to

PTA meetings, volunteering at community events and writing our next novel!

Doing great things takes a lot of energy. The commitment to do something great must be made on a daily basis. There are so many little things in life directing the flow of your energy downward- be it depression that we already mentioned or chronic anxiety that rationalizes your lack of progress.

How many times do we work with chicks that get all *precious* about the details—they've got all the answers as to why they're unhappy, why they're under-evolved, why they're still making 20K per year and with the most abusive guy in the universe---

It's because they're freakin' lazy. Not because they didn't get the on the Homecoming Court. It's because they channel all their energy into *thinking* about things rather than *doing* them. They are all thought and no action and pure laziness. It's because, no matter what the circumstances these chicks would still be unhappy because they are fundamentally LAZY.

Flyover Gals are supergirls. They are fundamentally raised to be about "action and results" and not about "chit chat and daydreams".

Circumstances don't matter to Great Women. When's the last time you read a biography of a kick-ass female and thought wowsers, her childhood was a real blast. All that poverty and illness seemed really entertaining, correct?

Ahem, you say.

Alright then. So let's **Ahem** a bit about Great Women… One of our favorite topics.

A Great Woman? Mother Teresa.

Mother Teresa did more with nothing than most nonprofits do in lifetimes with bucket loads of financial resources.

A Great Woman? Oprah Winfrey.

Oprah refrained from languishing in low economics and drug addiction and rationalizing her potential inertia because she was "underprivileged".

It is your responsibility to get moving, no matter what and a Great Woman practices this in her daily living...

It is your responsibility to get over your stuff and begin to inspire others because <u>inspiration</u> is what the Great Woman <u>does for a living</u>.

Circumstances, abuse, poverty and contempt are opportunities for the evolution of the Great Woman. She has ceased to see the negative as a road block for growth. She is the proverbial tree growing in the thick of the pavement.

When we were struggling with inertia and fatigue we would approach the Great Women around us- women that seamlessly juggled careers, kids and creativity... Women who were the elders of our Sexy Mama Tribe... We would beg them for the wisdom to crack our apathy and destructive tendencies. And more often than not, these Great Women would tell us--

"You know, sweetheart, it was just a bunch of baby steps to making my first million...."

Or

"Life required me to look beyond what I thought I was and begin to live in the knowing of what I could be in order to get the life that I wanted and that God had planned for me..."

In speaking to our elder tribeswomen we learned that we could benefit incredibly from zeroing in on our specific goals and taking the tiny steps toward that goal minute by minute, second by second.

We also learned the value of forgetting everything we thought we knew about ourselves and starting from scratch, in a co-creative process with the Universe.

This was the recipe for our success, loves. And it can be yours, too.

We want you to become obsessed with *your lives,* just as the Great Women are. **We want you to become alive in every way imaginable.** We want the pain of daily living and the slings and arrows of yesterday to be positively re-framed toward your goal of evolving as a woman, girlfriend, wife, mother, sister, friend, aunt, step mother and/or grandmother.

We want you to adopt our Manifesto and set aside the excuses. You will then live authentically… no masks, no b.s., just you.

When you get busy with improving upon you there just aren't enough hours in the day to sit around feeling sorry for yourself.
Life is simply too grand to bitch.

> **Helpful Hint:** Start a dream map that you post in a highly visible place that you refer to.

The Liars

If you don't think you do any Fat or Lazy Activities then you are Lying to yourself.

Stop it.

We hate liars. Men hate liars. Face it, you hate liars too… We all hate liars and yet women fall naturally into Lying Activities as a way to make themselves feel okay about the life they are manifesting around them.

Are you lying to yourself right now? You know who you are ladies!

You might lie to yourself about a current relationship. It's going to get better, right? Or, he isn't THAT bad. Perhaps you are lying to yourself about your own state of happiness and just going through the motions of life each day that have been laid out in front of you without challenging them and saying "this is not what I want".

Puh-leeze stop lying to yourself.

Challenge yourself everyday to be honest in your actions, thoughts, feelings and emotions especially towards yourself. If you can't be honest with YOU, then how can you expect anyone else to be honest with you? Respect yourself enough with honesty so others know your standards.
We were raised with strong family and community values and taught that lying activities damage our core. They allow us to be something we are not, to do things we do not believe in and subject ourselves to events and people that are not good for us.

Sexy mamas do not lie. Sexy women rely on the truth. Sexy mamas are authentic and insist on knowing themselves better each day and the only way to do that is through honest dialogue. You want to be sexy, don't you?

Ask yourself what you are lying about today and put a stop to it. It's ok if you have been doing it. We have all fallen victim to it. We lie to ourselves almost out of habit. You are your worst critic and you are you biggest champion. Do you have a voice in your head that criticizes you? Does she tell you "you look fat in that, you'll never succeed, you are stupid…..". Today, we want you to tell the critic in you to shut the eff up and allow the champion to emerge!

Lying sucks. Lying to yourself sucks more.

How often do we resign ourselves to some predestined fate?

How about we save the acting for the theater and get real with our living.

If you decide to have kids you won't resent the time spent raising them. If you decide to have a career you won't resent the time spent pursuing it. If you decide to have a loser friend you won't resent the time spent listening to her.

We're all big girls, now. We don't have obligations anymore. We have responsibilities and choices.

Ahem...

You are not obliged to martyrdom just because you're a freakin' female.

Martyrdom is not brave. Martyrdom is dishonest because most of us are not saints; we're tremendously fragile human beings. And martyrdom, ladies, is subscribing to the belief that life is a vale of tears and you have no personal *agency*.

You have *agency*, girlies.

You have more freakin' *agency* than you know what to do with. That's why you're frightened into a state of immobility.

You are undone by the immense possibility before you and the responsibility that comes with it.

You're fearful because you have no identified higher power that can guide your life in an effective way and serve as a source of energy when you're fatigued.

You want to believe what everyone else has told you because then you could predict the future. Sure it's a darker more depressing future but at least it's predictable.

Who has time these days to figure themselves out? Certainly not the martyred female species!

Whatevs, we say.

To follow your heart is the most efficient path to peace and prosperity for you personally and the world at large. You will not manifest great things if you are lying in the process. You will not be a part of great solutions for saving this planet if you are lying to yourself.

When you take the time to get honest, from the inside out, you become ten times more effective out there- in the real world. You radiate resilience. You radiate great strength. You become a magnet for like individuals- capable mates, capable friends, capable circumstances.

Example: How many of us make New Year's Resolutions only to capitulate one week into it? Is it cuz we lack the time? Nah. Is it cuz the gym membership costs too much? No way. It's because we are afraid of becoming. Who the hell are we to be strong and capable of defending ourselves? Who are we to be beautiful and stand out? We're so much better at denying ourselves and continuing to tell the awesome power of the divine to back off. We just love to hold onto our old pain. If we run that 5K then we're going to have to deal with the reality of our physical and emotional selves rather than the fiction we carry in our minds.

This is your life.

You can make of it what you will.
We advocate that you get busy with Becoming this instant.

There is no better time than now.

And when you get busy with living instead of dying slowly, you become productive.

You need to be productive in order to fulfill your purpose in this world and advance the human species. When you consistently engage in activities that are outside of your purpose you will burn out. You will manufacture disease. You will lose interest in growth, in initiative. You will become rigid and inflexible. You will enlist in the Society of Gutless Wonders.

When productivity becomes more important than your immediate emotional and physical needs, you will become the person you are meant to be.

Your life today is an amalgamation of what you thought you deserved yesterday. And if you were lazy yesterday you will reap the lack of rewards today. If you are productive today, you will find out what that productivity can yield tomorrow.

Helpful Hint: Start a "Quit It List" that you refer back to weekly that specifically targets the things you're going to stop doing. Resist the urge to get flowery and descriptive. Just spell out the facts, girls. And then get busy in the doing. If you are currently engaging in something that does not serve your body, mind or spirit in a healthy way, effing Quit It. And hurry up with it already. We need you in your strongest form, unhindered by *stuff*

The Dirty Word

Sexism. For most women, it's a dirty word.

The Theys (smart types) like to tell us that sexism is the reason that we, as women, lead such miserable lives and that were this horrible phenomenon to be eradicated, as in women and men were viewed as social and biological equals, then all of the world's ills would be solved.

We Midwestern chicks beg to differ.

We're a bit more empowered, 'round here.

Circumstances are merely hidden opportunities for the Sexy Mama, remember?

Therefore, **sexism**, as an inevitable circumstance that evolved from men shaping the institutions that comprise world as we know it, **is the best thing to ever happen to the wickedly intelligent and sexy woman because she knows how to navigate it.**

For all you overachievers out there who seek to remind us of the existence of the 24 hour work day we will concede that, yes, we too have been in your shoes. We too were hoping for the opportunity to tear the system down, rebuild it, have kids, be in a relationship, have the career of our dreams and go on lots of vacations. Then we realized there simply weren't enough hours in the day, and even if there were, the amphetamines required for such a lifestyle would get addictive eventually.

We found that the mantle thrust upon us by our academic forbears was just a little too much. *So we decided we'd rather be happy than right.*

Sexy Mamas Of the Midwest   44
Dallas - Stapleton
Guide To Gardening Your Soul

Cuz, isn't happiness what we are after in the first place?

There is nothing attractive about oppression and certainly nothing that makes us want to be magically transported to pre-lib days. However, we'd rather not talk about differences until the wee small hours of the morning and hang onto our "otherness" with clenched fists.

We like our lifestyles here in the Flyover states.

We could've had high-powered city-girl careers. We're both extremely driven, talented and capable. But, we traded that in after a while to come back to our roots and settle for a less stressful, more laid back approach to living and enjoy the differences between our sexes that is afforded in our smaller towns. We still have "power" but we yield it in ways that appeal to us and keep us happy.

We know men have certain advantages in our world. Whoop-de-doo. Women only recently got the vote and the benefits of birth control. Come on now; tell us something we don't already know.

We are not going to labor under the misapprehension that 35,000 years worth of evolutionary history will be shifted by a few decades worth of self-knowledge and good intentions in the actual day to living of today.

And, what we're most concerned with is the <u>reality of day to day living</u> in a world that, at times, minimizes our participation in it.

So we have to work a bit harder because society wasn't fashioned by women. Big deal. So we have to go through pregnancy and childbirth and get shoved out of the workplace with lack of benefits. While that may stink for most, we're not preciously clinging to our pain. We're personally grateful we aren't men and that our bodies are designed for things other than hunting and gathering.

We see the value in getting together with women to celebrate our hard work, our children, and our remarkable abilities. We're figuring out what makes us happy despite all the literature that says we shouldn't on the basis of our genitalia.

We are prepared to say "thank you" to the pain and suffering as it is <u>our direct path to happiness and grace.</u>

Don't men always say "no pain, no gain?" What the heck do they know? They are not half as strong and capable as room full of like minded women!

Funny, though the same men that speak of this pain wouldn't last a month pregnant and if they had to push a 7 pound human out of their penis, they'd scream for their mommies.

But we digress. Men are not our problem. We are. We want to blame our lack of personal integration on external structures like patriarchy when it quite simply isn't that case. Ask yourself honestly, please, would you be integrated mind, body and spirit even if externally oppressive structures were eradicated? Or would you, like so many of us continue to oppress yourself because you fundamentally suffer from a lack of self-love?

All we have to do is to look at the state of men in this country to realize that EVERYONE is having issues with self actualization, even the men among us?

So what's the big problem here?

The big issue is that we, as American women, have forgotten what it means to relate to the American male. We, as women, have forgotten the inherent power in our femininity, not as a means of manipulation but as a device of unique vibratory energy.

Men love women and women love men.

Sexy Mamas Of the Midwest   46
Dallas - Stapleton
Guide To Gardening Your Soul

And... Many times men love men and women love women. More power to them! Let the love shine on... There is plenty of room for everybody to *get it on* in the most authentic way possible. Whatever that means to you is your decision. For us, as predominately heterosexual chicks, that means one thing. For you it may mean something else. We love you nonetheless.

Please know this. We seek to unify the whole playing field between divisions that comprise this planet and encourage you to remember the Big Picture of what this book aims to do: get you to a place of self love so that you might more perfectly love another be they animal, vegetable or mineral.

So we ask you, what is wrong with being "taken for granted as a female" if it teaches you something about our divine purpose on this earth? What is wrong with being criticized if you learn to grow from that criticism? Why do we insist on limiting ourselves with concepts of how a mother, worker, or daughter *should* be? Why don't we start heading on our unique path? What is holding us back?

It is up to us to get quiet with ourselves and figure out how truly limitless our female energy is. Can you even imagine the amazing things that could take place if a bunch of us got together at a national level for massively loving systemic change a la Rose Kennedy and the Americans with Disabilities Act?

Ka-blam!!!

So dah-leengs, as two women who have been through it, we are here to encourage you to conserve your energy that you previously channeled into anger at "the system" and reframe it toward acceptance and love for the under-evolved parts in us all... Man, woman or child.

We are here to push you toward chucking away the big myth of female powerlessness and wake up to your birthright as an empowered human being who happens to have a vagina.

After years of being told that you don't have the power you start to believe it. There's a psychological term for this condition and it's called "learned helplessness." So it's time to get down to brass tacks and stop allowing the hate mongers among us brainwash our inalienable right to grace.

Helpful Hint: Traditional roles can be tremendously sexy. Next time you get the opportunity put on a strip tease for your man after you both get off work and watch his eyes bulge out of his head. Make dinner for him from scratch and watch him lap it up like ambrosia. Men are not abstract thinkers like women and benefit greatly from our ability to construct and produce a living fantasy. If you take a basic concept like a striptease or a home cooked meal, two very present items in popular culture that men freakin' adore and then add your characteristic female creativity to it - **Ka-blam**. Talk about an unforeseen

What are we advocating? A sense of playfulness and humor, ladies. Let's shrug off all the wordy yokes of yore and get back to basics.

Let's start falling in love with being a woman of our own choosing, whomever that happens to be.

Let's start loving the ability to choose the kind of woman we want to be today. It is a choice, remember.

When you choose who you are as a woman instead of throwing your arms up in a powerless sigh, you will find yourself edging closer to the sexy mama you are intended to be.

The Quest for Faith

How many of you know a gal who uses her religion as a disguise for what are, predominately, illegal or immoral activities? Perhaps she's stealing money from the PTA or collecting drunk driving charges on her way home from the Miss Congeniality pageant. We're sure you've heard about the sweet little church lady taking up the collection basket before the congregation and stealing from it behind closed doors. She's somehow able to justify her colorful predilections with her faith. These chicks are not the chicks we want you to emulate. These chicks are not real girls and therefore are not possessors of real faith.

The sociopathic zealots among us have a faith of convenience. You can't believe one day and not the next or be inherently good one day and evil tomorrow. Why be a protector and nurturer today and rob your congregation blind tomorrow? This is not genuine faith. Simply put: If you only have a "faith" when it suits you or when you are getting something out of it, then what is the point?

We learned a different way of life around here. In Flyover country, our faith is just as important as our family and our friends and betraying our faith would be just as bad as hurting our loved ones.

We worry about folks who parade themselves to the pretty church, quote scriptures and then are willing to gossip about their neighbors, shun their family members, etc all in the name of "they aren't as good in the Faith as us".

When did having real faith, real spirituality become something measured by members of a group?

We want you to be deeper than that. We're here to encourage you to truly believe. In believing, you will find your authenticity. We want, more than anything for you to be an authentic being. Let's all get back to our Flyover values and dig deep for our souls.

We want you to be the **same authentic creature** with the same authentic feelings toward everyone and everything. Same face to work buddies, same face to kids, same face to your parents, and same face to your mate. Same face to G-D. Because that's what being genuine is. Being "same faced."

But before we start off to the races, let us state a simple fact: authenticity requires faith. Faith in something bigger and badder than little ole you.

You're thinking, "oh crapola". These chicks are Born Agains or something and they're going to try to brain wash me into some sorta cult.

Hardly.

Rita is a working mother of four, former Catholic school girl and a bit too practical for cults.

Jessica is an ex-cocaine addict with a big mouth who the cults wouldn't have anyway.

So listen up. The short version is this. You need a Higher Power so that you can have a better quality of life. The folks who tell you otherwise are just lobbying for your increased misery so they have some company. Everybody needs a break from worry and fear. You can't write life's novel all on your own. That's what a Higher Power can do for you.

For Rita, her Higher Power is Jesus Christ. She was raised in the a small Midwestern town in a Catholic family and was taught Christ is her Savior. She refers to him in prayer and writing as God, Savior, Lord, Emanuel, G-D, Healer, Comforter, Father.

Jess finds her Higher Power in kinesthetic terms while moving through yogic postures, a 5 mile run or dancing with her infant son. For Jess, G-D is a feeling, a presence that fills her with a sense of bounty and security.

So go find one, girl.

The Smarties and their Lame Parties

Many folks don't want to believe. They'd rather be right. Then when they're facing the blackness of the nonexistent hereafter they can say to no one and no thing...

"Gee am I glad that I never wasted my time. "

Boy, way to be right.

We have one thing to remind those without any faith...You'd better be damn sure you are right, because if not, you are screwed.

When folks find out we're into the spiritual we often feel like our IQ's drop a few points in their minds. Sort of the same as when they find out we're from Ohio. It's like we're the kids who still believe in Santa or something.

Oftentimes, it feels like all the smart adults got together and got collectively pissed off at being deceived as children. Sure don't want to waste your time believing in something that isn't real like Santa Claus. Gosh darn it, we all believed and then we found out the truth, and just you wait---- we're going to find out the same thing about the Man Upstairs. He's just like Santa Claus, the Easter Bunny, The Tooth Fairy, and all those myths that our parents told us to make us compliant. God's just the same.

What a pile of putrescence.

We're not hell bent on getting you to believe in some personified old man in robes sitting on a throne. That's not how we get our rocks off. Neither one of us is hell bent on converting folks to organized religion because religion doesn't always encompass the spiritual nature of what we're interested in.

You may resist faith now because of where you started out. Don't let past experiences stop you from trying again on YOUR terms.

What we are into, as women who have minds and faiths of our own accord, is the encouraging of **individual spiritual experiences** that keep our readers wanting to get better, help more, and sleep a bit more soundly at night.

Your Higher Power doesn't need to be the God Almighty of Your Horrific Childhood. That's why we're going to take a cue from the Jewish faith and shorten the concept of a Higher Power to G-D. Your higher power begins with G and ends with D and whatever happens in between is your business.

Jessica likes to think of G-D as her Higher Self who is timeless and unlimited by physical form. This works for her as effectively as going to mass, prayer and meditation works for Rita. It is all about enhancing your personal effectiveness with an increasing ability to problem solve the under-evolved areas of your life.

And in the business of being straight forward business women, here are some more reasons why you want a G-D in your life:

To increase the distance between emotion and reaction so you stop behaving like a hormonal nightmare.

To transform the negativity that you encounter on a daily basis.

To remain hopeful and energetic.

To become your highest calling of self.

To believe in something bigger than yourself.

To cut ties with the past.

Those with great G-D's are the folks who accomplish great things in this world because they are in love with their G-D and it isn't a freakin' man, it's a freakin' positive spiritual force. There is plenty of room for Goodness to move in them and direct the daily lives of women with G-D's because, at their center they're obsessed with perpetuating good in the lives of all, not perpetuating good in the life of one (some man). How beautiful to have a relationship with your G-D such that you don't need to look to a man for your comfort, inspiration, affirmation and validation. You have that already from your G-D.

Life becomes a great adventure because their G-D transforms the contents of these women. Their G-D can transform any circumstance of negativity into an opportunity for buckets of spiritual development. These chicks can forgive. They can thank their oppressors, in due time, for lessons learned. They can shed more skin of self in search of more space within, more opportunities for love and forgiveness to move into.

LOVE is what your G-D brings you.

LOVE is what you are making room for.

And LOVE, darling girls, is entirely grand.

It isn't the buoyant flush of first romance. It is far more sustaining. It is grounding. It is connected. It is calm. It is stable. It is not something that you have to grip with both fists closed tightly. It is something that always is. Something that you can be patient with. Something that you can allow into your very being as a source of nurturance and transformation.

LOVE is limitless. It is peaceful.

And when you feel this love inside of you there is nothing that any man can do that will change that loving stance.

Every woman has needs that she wants met. I'm sure a lot of you by default tend to look towards the men in your life, or your friends or possibly a family member to fill up that well when it goes dry. It's natural to seek out people and expect them to start filling up our bucket with sand until it is overflowing again and we can feel like ourselves.

You will learn along the way that it isn't other people who can offer your soul peace and shelter. When you've lost your vision and are going backward, it isn't a man who is going to help you find your way.

The path darlings towards gardening your own soul and finding your authenticity begins with a relationship with someone greater than yourself, greater than any man and stronger than any person.

For many of you, that relationship may already exist, or perhaps it exists in the state that we call "pray and run". Call out to your higher power only when it is truly necessary or the chips were really down.

Let's stop treating our Higher Power relationship like a distant relative. No more "pop in visits".

This calm stable relationship with your G-D will help you call your soul back and be your unconditional source of support and inspiration.

This is not something that even Brad Pitt can compete with. Cheesecake and languid nights over a glass of wine beware. This is nothing that a 16" waist can compare to.

LOVE is your true essence.

It's what you've been chasing your whole life. What you've been mistaking as missing in your world.

It is you. Imperfect perhaps, but perfectly loved.

And when you feel that quality of LOVE that peace and ease in your daily living through the act of increasing and deepening your internal space there is not a single circumstance that can change your knowing. We cannot emphasize enough the change you will experience when you clear your heart and fill it with good.

You are truly a human being having a spiritual experience. Your G-D is the part of you that is eternal and unaffected by the entire surface bru-ha-ha. Your G-D can be anthropomorphized via religion or traditional models of God if you so choose, just as long as your G-D *encourages you to perpetuate in a state of LOVE.*

Your true peace and ease will come from directing all energy toward the pursuit of the space within. That space within is LOVE, is your G-D, is your Higher Power, is your truth, and is *incredibly individual.*

When you exist in a state of LOVE you are in essence **fearless** because you don't need anything other than your G-D. All relationships in the human plane will naturally fall into place. You will attract quality circumstances and people. You will arrive at center with a profound lack of emotional baggage.

Here's a great example of what a G-D can do for you. About 6 months ago, Rita lost her job. She'd been with the same company for five years, in an upwardly mobile capacity. Her family count on her income in addition to her spouse's to support their 5 school age children. She has 2 mortgages, 2 car payments and an infant to boot. When she found out her income was compromised she could've flipped out and guzzled a box of wine and some somas but no... Not our girl. Our girl was reminded of how much she needed her G-D. She knew her G-D didn't break promises to her. She trusted Him to write the novel. She hopped in the boat and went for the ride. She upped her spiritual ante, took her fears to her G-D who was big enough to handle it and wouldn't you know it... By trusting in a Power Greater Than Herself with her hopes, dreams and fears, she became pointed toward her highest good and is now in a position with a higher salary, less hours and was inspired to write this book with Jess. That's the thing about having a G-D. You build your faith and trust and you are able to let go and clear your spirit of worry. Those worries can be so harmful to your soul. Your G-D helps you maintain your clean soul.

Having a G-D is a lot like tending a seedling. A seedling needs space for its roots to go deep into the ground. A seedling needs nutrients in order to bear eventual fruit. A seedling needs to selfishly attend to its own needs at first, in order to survive. It needs to come in constant contact with its G-D, the earth, in order to flourish. It cannot flourish if it is focused on all the other plant life surrounding it. The seedling gets to work digging deep and nourishing itself. The seedling trusts its G-D to fulfill its needs.

Newsflash: Find G-D, whatever that means to you. A garden, your children, your work, the small still voice within, something at your center that instructs you on the deepest of levels in your fundamental worth and goodness. A sound G-D sustains you through the highs and the lows. A sound G-D is a positive influence that adds to your quality of life.

Helpful Hint: If you're unsure of what you want, make a Want Ad for G-D. Here's a copy of the one Jess has on her bathroom mirror...

29 year old woman in search of a Higher Power. Please contact telepathically as a testament to the following qualifications if interested:

- Creator and creative
- Relationship-oriented
- Monstrously *loving*
- Capable of slaying demons
- *Reliant & responsible*
- *Clever & freakin' hilarious*
- Can live in a confined space for the time being
- Humorous approach to defiance in followers
- Extraordinarily capable of the expansion of mind, body, soul
- Possessing of power, resources & abundant peace
- Unyielding to prejudice, obstinacy & hatred
- Sane, grounded, level-headed & brilliant
- Fantastic parent
- Forgiving
- *Patient & kind* since the beginning of time

The Four-Letter Word

It is a fact that the quality of LOVE you get in your interactions in the spheres of work, family, relationships are reflections of the love you show yourself. Perhaps you have more love for yourself in one of the spheres because it is a more authentic representation of who you are.

As women we often grow frustrated with our lack of being. We're not okay with becoming or blossoming sometimes. We're often impatient. We start to generalize one state of being as an overall quality, one that reflects our true character.

So many women come to us because they understand that they've got a pattern going with men. They keep picking the wrong kind of man, time after time. A broken "picker" is an epidemic across the country and not just isolated to our edge of the woods. And after lots of therapy and soul searching the big WHY most women come up with for this misguided monotony is that they have "low self esteem." And perhaps they do in the area that has to do with being able to successfully get the same quality of love they put into the relationship from their men but we would argue that this is one area and is not representative of the entire landscape. These chicks are generalizing the amount of love they get in one area across the board.

Self esteem is often essentialized into one measurement (good/bad) and generalized across the board (every area of your life). Certainly you can think of how limiting that is for today's woman who is an amalgamation of roles:

Worker

Mother

Sexy Mamas Of the Midwest   58
Dallas - Stapleton
Guide To Gardening Your Soul

Sister

Student

Wife

Girlfriend

Perhaps you feel empowered in one area (work) and disempowered in others (daughter). It is rare that we encounter a woman with truly low self esteem (across the board, every area feels shitty about herself). Let's think of why: perhaps you are applauded at work (high) but put down by your parents still at age 40.

Perhaps you are essentializing one quality of esteem across your entire view of self.

Use one of your spheres of empowerment to see how you are reflected and if it is an accurate representation and use it as a jumping off point.

If you are highly functioning in one sphere what would it take to broaden your functioning into another area? How are you more accurately reflected in one sphere as opposed to another?

We become more alive when were are loved. Love inspires feeling. Love heals old wounds. Love gets us to move beyond the limitations we thought we had, the limitations that we incorporate as "us." Love gets us to move toward a more accurate representation of who we are in our G-D's eyes. We are so loved by the Goodness that Permeates All Things.

Love may not be the panacea, but it certainly is a better cocktail than cheesecake, cosmos and complaining.

Limitations (poor esteem for self and others) are simply places where love gets stuck and cannot move more fully through. The highly esteemed person is an open channel. She is an open conduit for her G-D. She is able to move with confidence because she is supported by her G-D and her G-D's love. She is also supported in the everyday interactions she has by the love of those around her. It's hard to feel loved all the time by something you cannot see (G-D) which is why it is so important to be loved by those we see in our daily lives.

The highly esteemed woman may have encountered difficulties, had parts of her love for self and others stifled but she has owned up to her part and is doing the next right thing to grow. Doing "the next right thing," a major principle in the recovery movement, is a deeply spiritual act that allows us to move beyond places where the love has gotten stuck and through experiences of failure and learned helplessness. You can remap your thoughts and sense of self efficacy by doing the next right thing. You can become a light for those around you because you have been transformed for the better through life experience and through communication and dialogue with G-D and those around you. You have kept moving, evolving; the love has not gotten stuck. When love gets stuck you become immobilized, you become frigid, you become angry at your lack of movement, you get depressed, you get lazy, you get fat. It is lack of love that separates you from others.

Newsflash: The most effective thing you can do is to keep the love moving. You keep love moving by keeping your promises. You keep love moving by keeping your integrity, by building it up through the action of doing the next right thing despite the pain of the moment.

Skip over the pain. Skip right over the thought of pain and plunge right into the pool. Skip over the folks who stand spectator-like telling you what you need to do. You know what you need to do. Eff them.

We are staunch advocates of cutting off the dorks and depressives who fail to nourish your love. LOVE is the alpha and the omega. LOVE, we would argue, is the reason we as women, are so obsessed with relationships.

We think, as women, that we can find our meaning and purpose within the context of relationships. However we approach them a bit broken and seem to attract the blamers, shamers, criticizers and gutless wonders to help us love ourselves.

What in the world can we possibly get from a gutless wonder that we can't already give ourselves? What in the world are we profiting from being with a Walking Nut Sack? How is our esteem for self enhanced by someone who thinks less of us than we already do? If you are having difficulty with the basic task of self love in the first place- please G-D stop having relationships with people who encourage you toward more of the same.

Skip over the pattern by getting into our 10 Steps for Gardening in Section II. Learn how to cut the story line. Learn how to try something different. Refrain from judging yourself and others. Try loving yourself. You will attract the same amount of love that you show yourself. If you treat yourself like fecal matter, then it is very likely your partner does as well. He is aware of your standards through observation and will seek to enforce them. Think about it, ladies, he knows what the expectations are. Seriously, think about this. If he sees that you are self-deprecating then why would he need to show you anything else?

G-D is the only one who can love you above and beyond your current expectations. No man is going to fill up that hole sufficiently. Trust us, we've tried. It's G-D shaped, not cock-shaped, dah-leengs.

That being said, why is it that we choose to see love within the context of a relationship with a man rather than a relationship with ourselves or our G-D? How effective would we be if we took the time to direct all of that outward striving inward? How effective would we be if we took the time to water and nurture our own dreams instead of our partners?

When we work on our ability to relate to ourselves in a loving honest manner, we de-perpetuate the likelihood of being able to do the same in our relationships with others.

Ask yourself truly: are you loving toward yourself? Are you increasing the amount of buoyant energy in your life? How about your relationships with other people? How are your family relationships, how are your friendships?

When all else fails and you are that bottom of the emotional well, it is love that pulls you back. It is love that gives you a place to live, that nurtures you. Love is the supreme spiritual element that we all need more of.

Passion comes as a result of doing what you want, what you naturally are drawn to. Passion is exhaustible. Love is not. Love is limitless. It is your source element. It is your connection to G-D and to all beings. It is a unifying force and one that should be treated with the highest regard.

Do not squander your love. Save it, store it, reserve it for the one who is worth your while.
We both learned this lesson. We have both given our love to someone who wasn't worthy of receiving it and in return we found ourselves in a constant state of seeking more. When you allow yourself to be with a partner who doesn't appreciate or nurture your love, you will almost feel as though you are dying of thirst. Your pores will dry up and your emotions will cry out for just any drop. This is a dangerous and vulnerable place.

That's where the notion of celibacy comes from. It's not some sort of relic of times past, it has just as much significance today.

When you conserve your energy, particularly your sexual energy, you can contribute to your healing in the sense that you're not squandering yourself, exhausting yourself. You can start to rebuild what has been broken in the past. For a monk who reserves his sexual energy for G-D, he then has more energy to build and effect positive change upon the world.

Preserve your energy. Love the ones you are called to love in a way that frames your strength. In a manner that structures your character. The women of the Flyover states have enduring character and values, which can be truly intoxicating if we allow ourselves to pull out our love and share it with those deserving.

It is up to women to rescue ourselves from the notion that we will find all that required in the context of a relationship. So many women we counsel fall prey to the revolving relationship door. They never take a rest and spend time alone discovering the world and love without a man around.

We need to define love and hold our relationships up to that standard and not the other way around.

How often have you heard someone say that it wasn't until they had a child that they knew what love truly was?

Unconditional love or love in the purest sense is hard to find and sustain in the context of a romantic relationship.

We don't have evil thoughts about our children, do we? Everything we do contributes to their betterment, their happiness, their quality of life. When you wake up in the morning they are the first thing you think about. You would give up your life for them. There is nothing that your children could do that would make you reject them. You may not like what they did but you will always be their parent.

How many of you can say that about your partner?

Your partner cheats on you? You're gone.

Sexy Mamas Of the Midwest   63
Dallas - Stapleton
Guide To Gardening Your Soul

Your kid lies to you? You forgive them.

How beautiful is THAT kind of love!

LOVE is wonderfully intoxicating. It is a roller coaster of endless length. It fills the hole inside of you to the point where you feel complete always now and forever. It doesn't have to end. Ever. LOVE is your birthright as a sexy mama and it is absolutely something you can give yourself.

Love yourself so you can love others. Love yourself because it is simple and necessary.

A Pocketful of Inspiration
Before We Get To Work

Women as Commerce is an oooooooold concept (dowries, feudal times) and not one that's entirely thrown out the window. You only have to look at Donald Trump's latest marriage to some late 20's model to figure out what's going on---commerce, not love.

We're here to discourage you away from the kind of exchange that is based on one kind of appreciation- an eye for the external. Why do we feel so passionately about this? Because even the smartest supermodel is still only a supermodel if she hasn't diversified.

Case study #1: Jessica's friend who is a degreed surgeon, certified in two specialties by the New York Board of Medicine. Her great claim to fame was not the number of boob jobs she performed or the lipo service she did upon the playboy bunnies of the world which gave her a pretty sizable fortune. Her claim to fame was the fact that she encouraged these women of one skill set (the pretty skill set) to diversify their interests. After she sucked the fat out of their thighs she coached them on the importance of investing their money wisely so as to avoid the pattern that so many of these chicks fall into—the trap of the lifestyle and the need to marry well in order to stay entrenched in it, especially when the dude in question is a complete douche bag..

Our point, yes we are coming to it... You want to be a smart girl first and a pretty girl second. And if you started out a smart girl, and need to, go on and purchase the pretty girl accoutrements. You are not diversified if you are sharp as a tack but buried in a casing of fat. You will, in the end have a leg up on the pretty girls if you can hit the gym while pursuing your MD. If you a pretty girl first you need to get yourself a goddamned education and some effing empowerment.

Sexy Mamas Of the Midwest   65
Dallas - Stapleton
Guide To Gardening Your Soul

Don't settle for the first rich dude who comes round and wants to knock you up with a kid and then cheat on you. Say no way José to the proponents of the parasitic existence. Parasites, regardless of how pretty they are initially, do get old and do need to learn how to support themselves.

What are we advocating?

We are in the business of looking at ourselves as if we were listings on the NYSE. We know that sounds odd after all the talk about empowering the spiritual self but it all goes hand in hand. Our system is about perfect integration of the spiritual, emotional and physical bodies.

Our spiritual selves are SO STRONG and CALL US to build our emotional and physical bodies to the level of functioning that the spirit eternally serves at so why are we failing to get more interesting and intrigued with the world around us?

We may present as "one thing" initially but if we have properly diversified our interests we will be of limitless depth!

Women who are born and raised in the Midwest are especially familiar with the concept of diversification. We didn't have the luxury of relying on our looks to get us through life or simply selecting one skill to move us into the future. We learned to tap into our creativity if we needed to expand our wardrobe, we learned to compete with our brothers on the playing field; we helped our fathers in the garage and our mothers in the kitchen. In other words, there were no clearly defined roles for us and when it comes to taking on the world, we are better prepared to take off one hat and wear another.

We all want to discuss the real stuff. The stuff that matters. Even men. But we need to do so in an environment that is trustworthy and safe. Men are by nature, hunters NOT gatherers and by nature will not launch into a full frontal expose without proper coverage. It wouldn't make sense for them to jump out at the lion without proper supplies-spear, support in case the lion decides to (gasp) defend itself. Men and women are much the same. He will show you his goods eventually, but first he wants to make sure that you, as a lion, aren't a completely rabid wasteland of codependence and lack of initiative.

So keep on digging. Keep on Becoming...

You want to be the whole package, darlings. Then, when the natural unfolding happens on both sides it's a good and wonderful thing that is easy to do and sustain within the context of a human relationship. How many times do women get inside the therapist's office and make excuses- I'm not happy because I lost my job. I'm not happy because I'm a single parent and my ex is a cheap s.o.b. I'm not happy because I'm oppressed by my society.

As previously discussed, happiness, grace and peace are inside jobs. They are forever helped along by external validation and a sense of assuredness in yourself as long as you are grounded in your sense of who you are. A sense of no matter what- I chose it- and it didn't choose me confidence.

The universe is unfolding as it should and you are an important and vital part of things.

The confidence with which you approach your own life today dictates your future success tomorrow. We don't need to complain. We are self-sufficient, strong and confident and we weren't born with silver spoons in our mouth like many others. Sexy Mamas have to approach life in a unique way. An approach that scoffs traditional media and society and says "eff you" this is me and I am going to be joyful and happy under my own terms. I don't need a man, a wardrobe or a bank account to make me who I am.

That sense of self efficacy ensures that good things continue to happen to you even in the face of supposed adversity.

Our Example: Ms. Heidi Klum. How many women stress pregnancy weight gain before during and after? G-D knows we did. We're sure you've read about women who hire surrogates to carry their children in order to prevent the pregnancy aftermath from happening. Our girl Heidi says eff all that and she's a freakin' supermodel who built her empire upon what she looks like. She believes, truly, that the miracle of her body is its ability to right itself after anything. We'd argue it's a miracle of her mind as well. She believes that her stomach will stretch and give to seemingly unnatural proportions to support the growth of her child just as it will assume its pre-pregnancy shape directly following. She's not stressing it. And by not stressing it she's allowing the universe's model of perfection to take place in her life. She believes that she is more than her body and so is she. She also makes no bones about getting up on the runway in practically nothing directly following. This is one powerful mother of four.

Part Two: 10 Steps to Gardening the Soul

Pre-Test

Step One: Grounding

Step Two: Trimming

Step Three: Reach for the Sky

Step Four: Fertilizer

Step Five: Tending

Step Six: Facing the Elements

Step Seven: Sustainable Growth

Step Eight: Beautifying your Surroundings

Step Nine: Building Community

Step Ten: Your True Plant Identity

Post-Test

What Type of Plant Are You?

We love the metaphor of Gardening of the Soul because this quintessential pastime from the days of yore allows even the most reserved among us to get down and dirty with our bad self. Many of us grew up in the Midwest and Flyover states and we are all too familiar with gardening and it's many elements.

We will detail our Gardening Steps next to represent the spiritual tending we are encouraging you to do, but before we get into that, we want to introduce you to our little Plant Girls.

In the tradition of Cosmo, Facebook and all other mindless brain candy out there that encourages us to let loose a bit... Let's have a little fun, shall we?

There are over 250,000 types of plants and, if they were women, imagine the personalities they would have!

Ever wonder what kind of plant you'd be if we were to interpret and define you?

Quick... name your plant.

Are you high maintenance, clingy, and in need of a ton of water and pruning?

Could you be stuck in a corner for weeks without any attention and do just fine?

Are you low maintenance and relaxed?

Are you and edgy plant and your existence in the garden stirs things up a bit?

How do you feel about letting others take the stage and you just being a backdrop?

Are you a lively plant? Do you bring energy to a room?

Are you colorful, lively and charismatic?

Perhaps you are the plant that everyone wants to bring to the party?

Do you blend in with a lot of other plants and provide good ground cover?

Maybe you one of those rare beauties that we all envy?

Don't worry ladies, there is room for all types of plants and the big rains will eventually come. But, perhaps you have a lot of unwanted bugs or pest hanging around and you don't know what to do about them and you have to take care of that first. Those of you who attract pests need to learn how to ward them off!

Or, maybe you know some people like this…. They are beautiful on the outside but dead on the inside? These are the plastic plants that have no substance. We all know a few of them, right?

All kidding aside. If you can gain insight into your true plant type and the strengths and weaknesses of that type, you can begin to know yourself. Knowing yourself is the greatest gift you can give to you and the fastest way towards creating better tomorrows.

Go ahead and flip to the back of this book and take the test on page 181 as a pre-test.

When you're finished, look up your plant type in our index. Please answer the following questions when you're finished and record them in a journal that you will refer to throughout this process:

1. Do you identify with your type?

2. How far off are we in assessing the plant you pretend to be?

3. Do you regret answering a few questions the way that you did?

4. Which plant would you prefer to be?

Step One: Grounding

Grounding is all about a G-D.

We've told you why you need one. We've told you how to get one. Now we'll tell you how to feel the kinesthetic presence of one.

The shortest path to feeling the presence of G-D in your daily life is meditation and prayer. Prayer can be aversive to some, so we're not going to get directive at this point in time other than to say that if prayer works for you, do more of it.

Prayer can also get a bit heady for nut jobs like Jessica, who are extremely orthopraxic (need to engage in the "right" practice). There is no correct way to approach your G-D other than to start doing it.

The problem with short, infrequent visits with G-D is you don't get an opportunity to practice prayer and meditation and you will perpetuate this "pray and run" notion we mentioned earlier. When we say step one is Grounding, we take you there in order to keep you there.

Grounding is about having a consistent soul-partnership with your G-D.

Progressive relaxation, the technique we are about to teach you, is pretty fool-proof and a means of decompressing all the acquired horseshit of the hour/day/year/decade and a method we both use to keep grounded.

Go get a tape recorder that you can refer to throughout your step work. Keep it in a safe place so you know no other beloved nosies have access to it (like your 14 year old son who's constantly getting into things and repeating them over dinner with the neighbors).

Refer to the Relaxation Script in the Index of this book. The words in bold are the components of your relaxation script. Record your voice reading the words in bold. You will be making a tape for yourself to play back for your practice.

Exercise One: Find a place where you can be alone for an extended period of time, where you will be free from interruptions

Early mornings are great times to initiate your practice. The house is quiet. Everyone is still asleep. The daily onslaught has not yet begun. Your mind is refreshed and open to exploration.

Find a safe place where you can feel warm and supported. Lie on the floor with a blanket to cover you and a pillow under your head. If you have issues with your lower back, you may also want to put a pillow in the crease of your knees, supporting them underneath, which encourages the back to sink more fully into the floor. If possible, turn off the air conditioning/heating/fans and allow for a fresh breeze to circulate through an opened window.

Play your tape. Allow it to run for the duration of the script. When the script ends, allow yourself to wander in that safe space you've created within, through the act of progressively relaxing your body.

Shortcut: All Meditation is grounded in relaxation. Meditation is floating in that safe space you've created within. If you can, attempt to stay in that safe space for at least 5 minutes per day. Rita refers to this as "Calling her Soul back". It is a way to breathe, relax and ask her G-D to help her soul stay calm and focused.

Inspiration: Jessica used to work in a residential treatment setting with troubled youth. Most of the kids were expelled from foster homes due to violent behaviors and severe mental health issues. Many were labeled oppositional and were viewed as "lost causes." Jessica's boss and mentor did not subscribe to this belief and encouraged his staff to explore alternative treatments with the kids, including the purchase of yoga mats. Jessica taught a daily movement class which quickly evolved into an extended relaxation class much in the same form as the script above. The kids were encouraged to bring objects with them to class that brought them comfort including their pillows and blankets. The kids went through an adjustment period where they slept, snored or ignored the techniques. By sticking with the practice of encouraging their body to relax in a supported environment, many of them were able to build the safe space within them and in doing so, lessened the frequency and duration of violent outbursts. In short, meditation worked where psychotropic meds and other "talk" therapies did not.

Exercise Two: Consider involving yourself in a mind-body practice like Tai-Chi or yoga which are supportive companions to meditation and relaxation. Yoga was first developed as a means of increasing comfort during periods of meditation. Yoga was viewed as a preliminary act to meditative stillness as the body is given enough time to work out its aches and pains so as to call less attention to them during the meditation practice. Perhaps you have a physical practice already that has a meditative quality like running or biking. Whatever it is, do more of it and do it now. A consistent physical practice builds the body to the point where it can comfort the mind during times of duress and vice versa.

Inspiration: We have a friend named Annie who was going through a period of extreme loss and grief. No matter what, she felt undone, all the time. She could not sleep; she could not eat, and could barely get out of bed in the morning. Annie's depression was so profound that she felt alienated from her G-D and unable to engage in the spiritual practices that normally kept her hopeful. The only thing that kept Annie going was the time she spent running every day. When we asked her about her running practice, Annie said that it was therapeutic for her as it was impossible for her to both run and sob at the same time. She would run 3 miles to her destination every evening and upon reaching it, would have her ovario-busting-breakneck weep-fest for five minutes before turning around. She would run the 3 miles home and upon reaching it, her mind would clear. The depression would return a little while later but the intensity lessened as she continued to connect to her inner stillness, her peace, her G-D through physical means. The rhythm of her exercise practice allowed her to release some of the sorrow and pain that she had been holding onto for years. It allowed her to gain access to her problem solving mind unhindered by the fear of her current financial troubles and pending divorce. When the depression passed after a period of one year, Annie found herself to be a bit closer to her true fearless and authentic self... Her sexy mama status. She didn't hide from her pain but she also didn't play in her sorrow just because she was used to it. She got busy with Becoming!

Shortcut: We do not advocate ending your day with "noise." If you have a partner or children, encourage everyone in the house to schedule some non-electronic time at the end of the day (no television programs, computers, gameboys, X-box, etc). Rita and her children like to turn on a "soundscape" CD or relaxing music. It is a nice way to regroup and come back to *center* before going to bed. The kids like to doing their reading, drawing or cuddling during this time.

Gardening Tip: Go the store and get yourself a little seedling to tend at home. If you can find your plant that you identified as your type in the previous quiz. Do some research online and see if you can create the most nurturing environment for your little self. Do you see any similarities between yourself and your type? If so, write them down in your journal to refer to throughout this process. What happens to your seedling when you play music for it? When you talk to it? When you ignore it? When you water it too much or not enough? Make it a point to engage in your relaxation practice with your plant nearby. Monitor its growth throughout this process.

Step Two... Trimming

What happened to you age 0-18 had very little to do with what you deserve as a boundless and limitless human being. Don't assume that the story of your youth is an accurate reflection of your inherent worth.

Stuff happens to everyone. *Stuff* happened to both of us too and we are happy to report that we came out on the other side. A lot of work was involved and we are both still in the process of removing the *stuff.*

Here's the great thing about *stuff*—which is our sexy mama lingo for the shit of life. *Stuff* can be eliminated at any time (pun completely intended).

Tibetan Buddhists call this concept "cutting the story line" and apply it their spiritual practice as a method of cognitive re-mapping, a term that western psychologists use to describe the same process.

Both factions (the Buddhists and psychologists) have one aim in common: to remove the past from the present so as to empower the individual to move in new and different directions, regardless of their imprinting or negative beliefs..

What's the advantage of cutting bow strings with our old storylines?

An increasing ability to live in the moment.   Living in the moment is freeing.

Even the greatest psychotropic drug can be undermined if our negative thought patterns aren't taped over with new concepts that are more healthful and accurate. Even the highest mountaintop of meditation can be diminished by old cyclic thought patterns.

The most potentially healthful among us are more often than not THE MOST OPPRESSED BY THEIR OWN *STUFF* on an emotional level.

Understand this instant that most of the negative *stuff* you tell yourself is a lie.

How can you become authentic if you have the lies of your youth spinning and twirling in your head?

Understand right now that you spend most of your life lying, from morning to night if your dominant mood is sad, mad or depressed. You are so much more than that sweeties. We are bombarded daily with lies from the media about what we should look like, think, wear, and we internalize these falsehood. We then combine this b.s. with our own crapola and whamo! We have a negative self-image that perpetuates a false image.

We need to resist the counteractive images. Reject them.

Please understand that in holding yourself back with negative beliefs you are practicing intolerance and demonstrating a lack of forgiveness toward yourself which limits your potential exponentially.

The lies screaming in your head are damaging your ability to cut the story line and live in the moment.

Perhaps you have the Know it all Voice "You'll never amount to anything, you are doing that wrong, you'll fail today, your hair looks terrible, you are fat… "

Or Screw it Voice "I'm quitting my job, I'll leave my marriage, I'm going back to bad, I give up…."

Or the Hateful Voice "I hate you, I hate him, I hate this, I hate everyone"

Or the Little Girl voice "Nobody cares about me, I just want some love, somebody hear me, I want my mommy"

Or finally Your Voice "I'm ok, I can do this, I'm ok, I can do this".

Quit It Now.

YOU ARE **SEEPING** VALUABLE ENERGY. Put away those strong negative voices and forgive those who made you doubt yourself, put you down and filled your head with the know-it-all, screw-it, hatred, little-girl voice and move on.

You are a beautiful perfect thing that has yet to unfold her resilient wings. Now is the time to shed the chrysalis of *stuff* that enshrouds you and build the emotional body to the point where it can communicate with the spiritual self who is, in the words of Sharon Gannon (our favorite yogini)… Boundless, limitless LOVE.

So, dah-leengs, let get on with the *ahems*…

Ahem…

- You are not the result of circumstances, environment or *stuff.*

- You are not your mother.

- You are not your alcoholic father.

- You are not a whore forever despite having spent some time in Whoreville during undergrad.

The fact is that you are a present day amalgamation of previous choices.

If you don't like your current representation, start making other choices.

Choose to stop lying to yourself by cutting the boring, miserable, downtrodden story line that justifies your continued frustration, rage and, depression.

You don't need us to tell you how to do it other than the simple instruction to QUIT IT NOW.

Exercise Number One: If a negative thought comes up, dig out your journal and track
that little old thought to its exponential fear-mongering proportions. Why? Because fear is fundamentally hilarious. We'll use the example of a reoccurring thought of Jessica's. When Jessica gets down on herself she tells herself that she's a toad. Watch us walk through the process...

Jessica: I'm such a toad.

[*The feeling of toad-dom has arisen. Her next step, if she has read any of the above, is to tell herself that it's a lie.*]

Jessica: I'm not a toad. I'm a human being... Wait a second, no I'm not human... I'm still a toad... Darn it this isn't working!

[*The absolute belief in toad-dom has permeated Jessica's day. This is not a matter of simply cutting the story line. Jessica needs to sit down and write her way out of it. Jessica will now create a thought map where she follows the belief to its ludicrous end, thereby engaging in our next skill set which is called "hilarious story telling." Hilarious story telling is one of the greatest tolls in the Sexy Mama Toolbox of Spontaneous Healing.*]

Jessica: I am an absolute toad. If left up to my own toad devises, this is what my life would look like. I will be discovered by others and ridiculed publicly for my toad qualities. No one will ever ever ever want to see me in all my warty goodness. I will be unable to support myself in the human world because I am an amphibian. I will be laughed out of my housing development. I will be forced to live amongst the other amphibious creatures in the swamp. However, I am a vegetarian and will not eat flies. I will become lethargic and die due to lack of nutrition, and will die unassisted by my toad peers in the swamp who think I think that I am better than them because I am a vegetarian."

[Please recognize how hilarious fear can be when you take the time to follow it to its exponential degree… Jess is advised to keep writing, so she does.]

Jessica: Flies will feast on my toad corpse but will be improperly nourished because I was malnourished during my toad life. Instead the flies will have to return to the piles of dog poop that are nearby.

[Do you get where we're going here? We're encouraging you to ride out the fear until it gets to unnatural proportions and you can see the humor in your destructive thought/feeling/belief of the moment. When you can laugh at fear it shrinks. Fear has absolutely no defense against joy.]

Jessica: And once I am dead and unable to help others even through my decomposing toad body that can't nourish anything I will be staring into the blackness. G-D won't even want me because I'm so soulless and nasty. I will wander the abyss between heaven and hell and ribbit away the rest of my days, without a body to inhabit

*[Are you laughing yet? **Fear is easily chased away when we can learn to laugh at it in a loving manner.** There is no way that Jessica is a toad and will die purposeless. The entire act of Jessica thinking she is a toad is just as inane as you our darling student, believing that*

you cannot support yourself and are predestined to wander the earth alone. Those beliefs are fear produced and fear mongering and a freaking LIES that keep you locked in a pattern. Start chasing down all your negative little thoughts/feelings/beliefs and discover the space in your brain that is left by their eradication. Discover how much power you have when you realize how much mobility you have in your life to make positive changes… And how much joy is left in its wake.]

Exercise Number Two: A lot of our most destructive thought patterns are revealed when we tell another our life story. Take a cue from Alcoholics Anonymous and start telling your tale as a source of healing but on a small scale and watch the spontaneous healing emerge as you reveal it. Take this opportunity to tell your life story to your handy dandy tape recorder and allow the story to naturally evolve as it is right now. Spend time in the areas that warrant your attention, gloss over other areas that appear less interesting to you in this instant. After you record your story rewind and listen to it. Listen to your story with fresh ears. Examine the arc of the tale and the sound of your voice as you tell certain events. Did you leave anything out that feels important to share right now? As women who have been through some *stuff*, we may get a little sing-song-y with certain *issues* and allow them to take more precedence over other more inspiring aspects of our journey. Are you doing this? Or were you self-conscious of this in the telling of your story and so you blunted or manipulated the authentic telling of this in effort to appear to be other than yourself? Do you sound like someone else in telling your tale? Is your mood congruent with the events you are telling? Or are you one of those dah-leengs who can talk about the most horrifying stuff without feeling any attachment to it? Are you noticing any patterns in this? Let's try something a bit different, shall we…**Begin to rewrite your personal narrative to reflect your acquired strengths** (perseverance, resilience, humor). Tell a new tale. A better one that more accurately reflects the person you are capable of becoming and then get busy with becoming. Remember the days when you sat on the floor of your bedroom as a kid and clipped pictures of the life you would have as a grown up? Even if you didn't do this as a child, or even if you already have, do it again and DO IT NOW. Clip pictures that inspire you and reflect the true narrative of the story you wish to tell but aren't quite there yet. Post them in a "dream book" section of your journal that you refer to daily. Look over them as you would a precious photo album. Linger. LOVE. Feel the joy of recognizing your internal warrior spirit who has survived and is capable of emerging compassionate through the most tumultuous *stuff.* Your hope and appreciation for your spiritual self will be infectious and your G-D will infuse that part of you with even more influence over the less developed, more fearful parts of your personality (i.e.: the little girl who is still afraid of the dark, the saboteur who wants you to do lots of drugs, the depressed teenager who wants to sit around all day eating potato chips, etc). When you acknowledge your spiritual self and appreciate her limitless, compassionate, fearless guidance, you begin to live more in her reality, which is an unending state of gratitude. Gratitude for what is yet to come is one of the most difficult things to pull off but is evermore important in this world that is increasingly fear-full and fear-based. The universe is unfolding perfectly and as it should. Your G-D has a good hold on things. Trust that this is so and your spiritual self, your internal supergirl, will begin to take over your life manifesting increasing levels of abundance until what you are living is actually heavenly and ceases to be martyred drudgery.Take this opportunity to begin to rekindle some hope about what life can hold for you. You can be anything you want as long as you continually commit to clearing out the old negativity and filling that empty space with new productivity.

Our example: Two years ago, Jessica was having difficulty getting pregnant. A reproductive specialist ran lots of tests and ultimately said she had a snowball's chance in hell of conceiving "unassisted." Jessica explored all the methods that science had to offer- all the needles, all the potions, all the facilitated deliveries of her husband's sperm to her eggs. The result? Nada. Jessica was a bit pissed at what she experienced as the financial equivalent of sticking cash in a Chippendale's jock strap and vowed that, were she going to spend that kind of money on a kid she should at least have better results in the end rather than a bunch of bruises on her legs from hormone injections. So she started looking into adopting and began visualizing the potentiality of having a kid on a daily basis by pasting pictures into what later became the "dream book" section of her journal. These images represented her as a mother already and were not representational of her as a woman who was trying to conceive and failing. She started waking up earlier as she would to feed and clothe a kid. She began referring to her backseat while driving as if there were a baby back there. She felt gratitude and blessings daily for the motherhood that she had, in practical terms, not yet realized. She began to feel peace in her heart and mind that this one area of her life was "solved" and that her G-D was going to take care of it. She let go of the problem as her own and saw it as "solved." She even went so far as to purchase a pair of black patent leather shoes for what she assumed would be a female. Why not? The world needs more women like us! G-D's answer to her dilemma? Her then-marriage fell apart, the two divorced, and Jessica wound up knocked up with her boyfriend of one month's kid. And just to prove that Jessica's G-D has a sense of humor, the baby was a boy. Jess continues to hold onto the black patent leather shoes, knowing full well that her G-D will deliver the goods as long as she continues to believe in the accurate story and is happily awaiting the female counterpart to her wonderful little boy… Or perhaps the realization at some point that her little boy is more comfortable in black patent leather shoes, if he happens to move along those lines. The important part is that her dream was realized. Ka-blam.

Short cut: Once the perceived problem is cognitively remapped through cutting the story line and believing in an alternate result the problem ceases to exist. The universe becomes capable of cleaning up what doesn't fit in ways that not even an award-winning novelist could have predicted.

Meditation: The Indo-European root of the word, forgiveness, means *to let go of anger.* Acceptance of irrational behavior propelled by the under-evolved is nowhere in the original definition so if that's your understanding of what forgiveness means, perhaps you should re-examine it. Forgiveness in our book simply means to let go of the toxicity of rage. There is so much bounty out there and even more importantly, there is so much problem solving capability available to you from your spiritual self and G-D once your emotional and physical bodies let something go. There is a Sanskrit saying, "Sat Nam" that embodies this concept of withdrawing your precious hold on someone or something, that when uttered regularly is believed to cause a cognitive shift in the utterer. Go ahead and Sat Nam all of the annoyances in your life. By doing so you will release your ties to what you think you are entitled to and you will then move toward your true destiny and true blessings.

Inspiration: Dr.Ihaleakela Hew Len is a psychologist who worked in a series of mental hospitals during the course of his long career. While doing chart reviews at a hospital for the criminally insane in Hawaii, spontaneous healings were noted to be occurring among the patients. Many workers noticed a rapid recovery for individuals who were previously regarded as "lost causes." Folks began to associate Dr. Len's presence with these individuals who were able to discontinue many of their powerful psychotropic drugs, re-enter the community safely, etc.... Folks also began to notice that staff turnover was decreasing and clinicians were showing up for work on-time and eager to help. It seemed that an immense positive force was filling the hospital. The most miraculous thing about this phenomenon was that Dr. Len never SAW any of the patients face to face. So what the heck was this Miracle Worker doing? Well…We told you already, silly… He was sitting in his office doing chart reviews... But here's the kicker, while reading over patient files, Dr. Len said to himself, in his mind, I love you... I am so sorry... Dr. Len chose to love and apologize to those aspects of himself that were in tune with the symptoms of his patients and literally dissolved all feelings of separation between these "lost causes" and himself, a degreed professional. Through the act of dissolving fear through love and acceptance and ultimately SELF-FORGIVENESS, not only did Dr. Len get better but the entire facility did as well. And that hospital went on to close its doors. This practice is known to native Hawaaiians as Ho Opononopono and is regarded as sacred in its application and effectiveness.

Meditation: When faced with a circumstance that seems impossible to forgive, let alone understand, join forces with your indomitable spiritual self, the one who has been there beside you all along and has witnessed your pain. Begin speaking to the broken parts within you the next time that old familiar agony comes up, in a familiar way, and state "I am so sorry…" You might want to engage in a mindless task like washing dishes while apologizing to the broken parts within you, stating that simple statement over and over. After some time engaging in this practice those old hurts will dissolve just like Dr. Len's and before you know it you will be transmitting loving energy to yourself and all who surround you. And if you find yourself wanting to kick your practice up a notch, engage in a challenging practice like running or serving others in a volunteer capacity while stating the apology.

Gardening Tip: Just as soil can be worn away and washed away by wind, water or man, causing malnutrition and stunted growth, so can the emotional self of the plant totem. When you find your emotional energy hearkening toward anxiety/frustration/rage/shame/blame/guilt or any other **seeping emotional energy**, practice a very simple yogic technique that seals the root chakra, known as *mulabhanda*.
By sealing the root chakra, through exercising our *mulabhanda* - you reduce your non-productive energy release that is so often directed toward negativity and instead conserve that energy for your own healing. How do you do it? Simple. The next time you feel your emotional self take off for the non-healing energy races, tighten up your kegel muscles as if you were trying to stop peeing and *imagine the kegels pulling up and inside you in an effort to stop urinating your healing energy.* Sounds funny, doesn't it. We think so too. But it effing works. By the time you release the kegels after a period of holding them securely and snuggly for a few seconds; you will feel a sense of peace and ease throughout the physical body. And then you realize that you just did it- you tricked your emotional self into

Sexy Mamas Of the Midwest   87
Dallas - Stapleton
Guide To Gardening Your Soul

wholeness using the beauty of your physical body and called it to hearken toward the perfect healing of the spiritual self, which is its perfect destiny.

Affirmation: "No matter how horrible it was, nobody stole me. In the end it is a great gift to be broken to bits as I get to CHOOSE forgiveness. I am free to build myself, mind, body and soul as I see fit..."

Step Three... Reach for the sky

Now's the time to begin filling the newly created space in your head that was previously occupied by false beliefs.

Fill it with big ass deliciously perfect dreams that you will realize. Revisit your dream book and look at what makes sense for you and what does not.

A word about dreams.

If you are practicing the art of energy conservation which you learned in Step Two, the inspiration faucet is going to start running 24/7.

We attribute it to not pissing away all of your energy on mindlessness. You've cut your old story-lines and now new adventures can unfold.

However, in pursuing our so-called dreams, we can still be a bit mindless, and so wevwould like to issue a few warning calls.

We all have the fantasy of the dude who sweeps in and makes our lives easier. Sounds romantic, correct?

In some ways, it would be. However, make certain your dreams do not embody the fat, the lazy or the lying activities previously mentioned.

Your dreams must move concordantly with your highest good. Your highest good wants you to be successful, productive, creative and effective.

Your highest good does not want you to sit around all day eating bon bons. (Lazy and Fat)

Nature abhors a vacuum, darlings, and what we are doing is moving in accordance with the universe's aim.

The universe aims toward perfection and wealth in all areas. The universe wants you to be ridiculously successful and effective with your Grace Given Talents (GGT's).

Both of us have walked away from millions of dollars in potential revenue from "marrying well" because the dude couldn't ring our bells.

In doing so, we preserved our emotional and physical selves through honoring our unique sexual energy which is intrinsically linked to harnessing your dreams.

When we were in bed with someone who rang our bells sexually, we found another energy source to feed us toward moving in the direction of our dreams.

So here's another a bit more of the most loving *Ahem*, since we're on the subject of men again.

Ahem...

A man's responsibility is to eff you properly and provide some modicum of emotional support.

A man is not responsible for your expense account or plastic surgery fund.
That is on you.

If you are moving in directional flow toward your purposeful course you will be ridiculously successful.

What is your purposeful course?

We can't say.

We can advise you to look closely at your GGT's, how they are manifested and then figure out where you are headed. You must know your GGT's and be able to state them freely.
If you are conserving your healing energy through the practice of the previous two steps, your GGT's will jump off the effing page at you. Your GGT's will lead you to your most fundamental baseline functioning- what you do most perfectly when balanced and at peace, something we like to call Your Lowest Common Denominator or LCD.

A word on the GGT's...

Rare Insight

Rare Insight isn't the result of education. Nor is education fundamental to rare insight. We know plenty of ridiculously MENSA eligible women who can't operate a standard transmission or tell us what causes a 2 year old to cry. We also know women with incredible wits who make better therapists to domestic violence victims than the degreed professionals.

In short, intelligence comes in all shapes and sizes, just like sexy mamas.

And if you are graced with the GGT of rare insight, you have the ability to turn on the truth faucet to others in the most effective manner. Perhaps it's not always the most loving and appropriate but returning to love is a skill we can advise you on. The GGT of Rare Insight can't be taught. You've either got it or are on the outs with it, right out of the box.

Insight GGT's are the women who are going to save the world. They have a lot of work to do but when out of touch with their truth, can manufacture issues like eating disorders or other addictions because they are directing their insight toward themselves rather than the world stage. We love Insight GGT's because, when in balance, they are fighting warrior women with the biggest most beautiful mouths on the planet. These are our artists, musicians, writers and hell-raisers. These are the women who remind us of our fundamental worth and integrity which is why it is oh so important for them to get their shit together emotionally and physically.

Joy

Are you an infectious personality? Do folks take on your moods and attributes freely and lovingly? Do you attract admirers and wealth to you like nobody's business? If you can answer yes to these questions, perhaps one of your GGT's is the quality of joy. Joyful girls are the types who attract men like ham sandwiches with their unique energy. They attract female friends like a Botox party. However, they can become energy sources for less-evolved others to feed off of. So, for the joy to last, they oftentimes need to retreat in order to fill the proverbial well and remember the source of their joy which is their connection to G-D.

An out-of-balance joyful girl is often the chick who is still effing the man with the little penis who kisses like a slobbery duck because she doesn't have the heart to leave him.

An out-of-whack joyful girl might perhaps over-donate to her favorite causes and find that a week before payday she's eating ramen noodles when there is no good excuse why.

Joyful girls are so resilient that not much can oppress them externally. However, they are very effective at oppressing themselves.

Remember, if you're GGT is joy, you are not helping anyone by depriving your self of your highest good. If you begin to manifest your dreams, you will serve as an even greater energy source to others.

Beauty

Beauty GGT's are so intoxicating because of their external attributes. Oftentimes artists or stay-at-home moms, Beauty GGT's are intrinsic to perpetuating the concept that balance is crucial to evolution. A CEO is a fantastic example of a Beauty GGT in that she is the gorgeous and highly imitated wolf mother of her pack, who takes care of her cubs (her staff) in the most graceful way she can. And because of her tendency toward grace and balance, others love to follow her because they feel safe.

Why do we love beautiful people? Because the spirit tells us that beauty is balance and balance is good.

However, we oftentimes mistake external beauty for internal beauty and we all know that to be a misrepresentation of truth.

We can tell you, as your fearless authors, that it is your effing birthright to be gorgeous. With a Beauty GGT, however, there is an otherworldly luminosity to her presence of which she is fully aware and protects an entrepreneur's mentality.

Entrepreneurs define success for themselves, not by some societal belief that was created for them. They are self-actualized, self sufficient human beings who break away from the pack and say "this is what I see for myself, want for myself and am going to get for myself". Beauty GGT's are critical in this movement toward self-actualization because they inspire the under-evolved among us with the soul song of balance.

If out of whack, however, Beauty GGT's can be some of the shallowest and stuck up personalities on the totem. They often mistake their external beauty for truth and get lazy about working on the internal beauty or vice versa and uh oh spaghetti o's... Recipe for disaster.

Energy

Are you an Energizer Bunny? Do folks fight over your time and love to feed off of your joie de vivre? Do men literally catapult themselves into your bed daily even when you're wearing your glasses and haven't had the chance to shower?

If so, you might be an Energy GGT.

And Energy GGT's need this *Ahem*, more than any other.

Ahem Lil Ms. Energy...

As an energy GGT, you need to begin to market yourself and not your vagina.
Vaginal Marketers are the kinds of chicks who like to quote other more interesting people rather than form their own opinions. Vaginal marketers would rather waste their energy than get going forming their own opinions. Vaginal marketers are friends of the Residents of Whoreville but don't consider themselves to be "as bad" because men flock to them and are powerless against their unique energy. That being said, Ball-O-Energies, as with all GGT's, you will age, grow less imbued with the said Energy and will need to learn to mitigate you risk or else fall victim to a nervous breakdown at age 80 when you're exhausted.

So Lil Miss Energy, start to consider the intelligence involved in giving your uniqueness away. Well, some companies do it, you say, as a means of attracting "new customers", but you are not out to get customers. You need your energetic value for yourself and Your

Sexy Mamas Of the Midwest   94
Dallas - Stapleton
Guide To Gardening Your Soul

Inevitable Becoming. Are you kidding yourself into thinking you are doing this planet any good by spinning your frenetic lil' wheels all day long? Get real with your lovely spazz self and begin to conserve you for you. An Energy GGT is a gift to the universe. She needs to begin to harness and direct her vibes successfully in order to soul charge the human race. She must figure out how to channel herself into service and teach the next generation of Vibratory Girls, otherwise she will burn out like the most distant star... Amazing potential but nobody got to see her.

Healing

These are the GGT's who grew up wanting to bear witness to others' suffering in order to give them the courage to heal.

These are the GGT's who endured upper level chemistry in order to learn the language of science and command the highest good in a field like medicine.

These are also the GGT's that bucked conventional healing practices and listened to their G-D to carve a unique path of their own to address their own healing and in doing so, healed a crap-load of broken others with their tales.

Healing GGT's are so freakin' powerful, but when selfishly listening to the song of their own pain and torment, can be an incredible obstruction to others.

Healing GGT's engage in acts of mending without even realizing it. You can be at the grocery next to a Healing GGT and suddenly your cough feels better. Why? Because a Healing GGT is an empath and her baseline is *to heal others*. Her spiritual self doesn't bother to give a heads up to the emotional and physical aspects of her when she's operating at her baseline of healing, which is why a Healing GGT may manifest bizarre illnesses and infections when she hasn't tapped into the unlimited power of her G-D as a parasite disinfectant.

Listen up Ms. Healing GGT… We know you know you are great. But most of the time, it is important for you to know that all successful healing acts aside, you can be really freakin' nutty when you are out of tune with your Grace Given Talent.

The healing act is not fostered by you. You are a channel for it to move through. The healing act comes from G-D and is an amazing GGT that must be carefully aligned with a woman who has the emotional fortitude to channel it without it making her ill.

All of your fun characteristics and likes and dislikes are exciting to others if you are fundamentally real underneath. You are not a real if you are crazy. You're just not deep enough. You're not a real healer just because you carry a stethoscope or have an amazing reiki practice. You are a healer because you are in touch with your vulnerability, address it and honor it daily and give thanks to G-D for your precious gift.

Take a cue from Barbie and G.I. Joe. Ever notice that G.I. Joe is always wearing the same clothes? He might get a new truck but he's still GI Joe. Golly. Barbie is a doctor today with all of the external accoutrements and a corvette steering bimbette tomorrow.
She ceases to be the same woman when she jumps into her plastic car.

Do not be so dissuaded.

If you are a true healer, you cannot take it off like a costume. It is your baseline as with all the GGT's.

So if you are a physician, a massage therapist, an optometrist, a dentist, a therapist, a social worker, it's time to start asking the big question… Who are you serving and who is your therapist cuz it's time, Miss Healer, to get yourself on the same path.

Our Example: We have both made the mistake of putting our dreams on the backburner because we were misled about our true GGT's. We often held tight to the excuses of "responsibility." After all, we were married, we were mothers, who were we to realize our dreams? However, you will reach the point one day, just as we did where it was a matter of either honoring that GGT or losing it and fading into the abysmal state of deprivation of inspiration.   We both came to realize that we were no good to ourselves, our children, or the men in our lives if we were stalling our dreams for the sake of other's happiness. Save yourself first. Take care of your own inner wealth and everyone around you will be better off for it because once in tune with your GGT(s) we could go about systematically sharpening them through honoring them and clearing the energy of yore that prevented their perfect manifestation. We could both continue to go to jobs day in and day out that served a financial purpose for our family, or we could do something that actually inspired us. We have found (and our families agree) that harnessing our GGTs makes the entire home a happier place.

 So many of us spend crazy amounts of energy on things that don't bring us closer to our dreams. We want you to channel your energy where it is needed—the perfect manifestation of your GGT's.

Shortcut: Take a look at your dream book and reflect upon what pictures hold the most content for you. Which images pop out in your head? Are there any reoccurring images that absolutely, categorically resonate for you? Who are the people that are in the pictures with you? What are they doing and saying? How are they treating you? Where are the places you are living? What are you doing? Modify your dream book so that it makes sense to you and is reflection of the world admiring you for your unique GGT's. Dream the Big Dream that your G-D intends. Manifest your GGT's.

Meditation: After you have engaged in your relaxation practice, take some time to imagine what your perfect life would look like in visual terms. Feel the feelings associated with it. Those delicious feelings are the means in which your G-D speaks to you and helps you identify your highest purpose. See yourself in the form that best represents your highest calling. Refer to these sensations daily in your meditation practice and give thanks to your G-D for allowing you to dream the big dream. Your gratitude will help you achieve it.

So having addressed the main GGT's: Rare Insight, Joy, Beauty, Energy & Healing let's get to our main project at hand, your LCD status, or Lowest Common Denominator, as we like to call it.

Your LCD is what happens when you shake up your GGT's like a martini. Remember loves, all of us have more than one GGT and that's what comprises your Lowest Common Denominator Status.

Reducing a bunch of numbers into a lowest common denominator is one of the first things you learned in math class. Remember those pesky things- they're fractions that can be divided by a whole number and as such, simplified into something more compact and travel-worthy. We know you were told that there wouldn't be any math in all this, but we brought you here for a purpose, dah-leengs.

Your LCD is a means of simplifying your complicated view of self. Your LCD will tell you where you lie authentically and allow you to spiritually soar. Your LCD unifies your physical, emotional and spiritual selves into a compact lil' number that can easily sneak past the Negativity Police. Honoring your LCD is the fastest means of achieving an accurate Big Dream or reevaluating an existing dream that is perhaps calling for revision.

Inspiration: Archibald Alexander Leach, better known by his stage name Cary Grant was one of the premier movie stars of the 20th century. We're here to tell you that this suave, debonair man did not start out that way, rather, he chose it. He was born poorer than dirt in a steel town in northern, England to a mother who was severely mentally ill and later institutionalized when Grant was 9 years old. Grant's father wasn't much help as a single dad and told Grant that his mother was on "extended holiday." Grant dropped out of school at age 14 and moved to America to pursue a career in the theater after forging his dad's signature on the paperwork. In the course of crossing the pond and making his way to Hollywood, Grant identified his goal (super-stardom a la Gary Cooper or Clark Gable) and went about making the necessary changes to make it happen. We like to think of darling Cary LCD's of Insight, Beauty and Energy in his unique ability to command the attention and affections of others. Cary didn't go to school for a gazillion years and attempt to do biochemical research. Cary didn't go into the priesthood. Cary made use of an accurate LCD and channeled his energy and balance into tremendous success, which is what is waiting for everyone if they honor their unique GGT's. Cary adopted an accent that hid his working class roots, changed his name, started sunbathing to appear well-traveled, and read up on the classics and foreign languages. Our little roughneck from Bristol successfully conveyed the bearing of a well-traveled gentleman with no role model other than his own wit and fortitude. This persona carried its way onto the screen and established him as which was Alfred Hitchcock's leading man. The AFI regards Grant as the second greatest film star of all time. Not bad, eh. But the ultimate compliment in our minds begins and ends in 007... Ian Fleming reportedly based the character of James Bond upon him... Bravo.

Gardening Tip: Don't be a parasitic plant, one which lives on, and acquires it's nutrients from another plant. Have your own dreams. Be your own, unique plant. Become a self-actualized woman. If you need to, go on a vacation by yourself. Sit by the beach, in the mountains, or by a volcano and feel the majesty of their unique grandeur. You are no less unique, Plant Girl, than the most beautiful monolith. Begin to honor your spiritual self by cleaning up the residual physical and emotional funk that is blocking your dreams. When your LCD begins to speak to you there is no mistaking its siren's song. This is the sound of the soul calling you back.

Step Four... Fertilizer

There is a theory in anthropology (science of studying people and cultures) that has been widely discussed in the last 50 years which basically examines the effects of observation upon a subject. In deference to the continuing upholding of Duh Science, anthro is now reporting that by observing something you change it. Tell us something we don't know, you say. Well, we're about to. Anthro nerds take it a step further- they call for a level of personal inquiry into observer's motivations... As in, what makes you, some sort of expert? They also assume a reflexive attitude; one that acknowledges that the observer can't possibly know all there is to know about a subject.

This attitude of reflexivity, doll-faces, will specifically apply to your examination of self, or persona that you cast upon the world.

You will miss things in your examination of self as you try to apply Cosmo magazine's latest top twenty tips. That's why we're going to give you a multi-valenced solution. Cuz you need plenty of fertilizer to become the best lil' plant you can be.

We grew up in the Midwest and while Cosmo magazine and the media will try to impart the wisdom of the world on us, we prefer to take a more rational approach to feedback.

When a kid goes into be evaluated for ADHD, everyone is given a short questionnaire to complete. Kid, Mom, Dad, primary teacher, perhaps a next door neighbor or family friend. The diagnosing clinician then compares the questionnaires completed by all parties and based upon his or her own personal observations of the kid in question, come to one of the three following conclusions:

(a)Yes the kid meets the criteria and is ADHD.

(b)No the kid does not perhaps it is something else.

(c) Inconclusive needs more observation.
The reasoning for such a thorough approach is clear. The diagnosing clinician wants to form an unbiased opinion of what the kid's baseline looks like as well as the behavioral issues when they arise. You don't want a little kid medicated for something he doesn't have.

We're going to do something similar with you.

360 degree feedback is a development tool used in business which enables a person to solicit feedback from "all degrees". The feedback helps the employee identify areas of strength and weakness. In those cases, the feedback is anonymous; however, the purpose remains the same. The feedback is going to be honest, straightforward and, if taken to heart, will provide an opportunity to take action and correct behaviors, adjust attitudes or alter perceptions that others have.

We are advocating our own method of 360 degree feedback which we refer to as Fertilizer. Think of this as a Fertilizer intervention! How are you going to honestly identify your weaknesses, highlight your strengths, set your objectives and begin your path towards becoming a self assured, confident sexy woman if you are only basing your perceptions on your own views?

If you grew up in Flyover states, you know fertilizer is necessary for growth, ladies, and you must get fertilizer in the form of feedback to get started.

Face it! Hearing feedback is tough. Sometimes it sucks and is harsh! What if they insult your hair, say your personality is obnoxious or criticize your wardrobe? Well, be honest with yourself. If all of those things are true and you have chosen to look blindly in the mirror, then you will never move past the stage and state you are in.

However, if you approach this as a personal development opportunity and remind yourself that a strong, confident, sexy woman will value feedback and will embrace it, own it   you will be on your way towards obtaining your personal goals.

It will take effort, but the return on your investment will be a life of self-fulfillment and no one can put a price on that.
Unlike in business, we are not going to allow the person(s) you solicit feedback from to hide behind their answers as "anonymous". It will not do you any good to receive feedback if you don't know who to go to for further clarification or more information.

Sorry ladies. You need to select people that 1.) You trust to provide you with the most honest feedback and 2.) That you know you can handle hearing this feedback from. Otherwise, you are wasting your time and you will possibly damage a few relationships along the way due to your own inability to value and accept constructive feedback.

We believe follow-up is crucial to the success of you taking in the fertilizer.

Ask questions, ask for clarification, and get more information. Do whatever you have to do to arm yourself with as much information about yourself so you can embark on your journey of becoming the best you can be.   If you need to change your appearance, behaviors or how you present yourself to ensure your future success, are you clear about EXACTLY what you need to do? Do you feel equipped to make the necessary changes?

If not, review your identification with G-D. And find one who will give you the strength to listen to others.

Exercise One: The Fertilizer tool we are going to have you utilize is a simple SWOT analysis. This will address your strengths, weaknesses, opportunities and threats.

Your feedback should come from 4-5 valued sources. One source should be familiar with you for the duration of your life (family/school friend). One source should be a work acquaintance. One source should be your hair stylist or someone that knows you on a superficial level. One source should be your best friend. One source should be a neighbor or babysitter who is familiar with your home life. One source should be someone who's objectivity you completely value (our example that we use a lot is your gay male friend). The point is you have information from the representative spheres of your life. Ask them to complete a SWOT analysis on you with the following descriptors. If you feel ready, share your dreams with them and ask them to reflect upon your SWOT's ability to align it with your dreams. Ask them to help you identify what you need to do to make your dreams a reality. Tell them that above all, you value the truth and are prepared to receive it.Strengths: These are the internal positives- your talents, knowledge, skills, and unique attributes. Your strengths give you a competitive advantage over others. These may include your GGT's. Weaknesses: These are the internal negatives; what holds you back and areas you can work to improve. A lack of strength in certain areas can be viewed as a weakness. Opportunities: These are the positive external conditions that you can take advantage of for profit and growth. Look at your strengths. Do these present any opportunities? Look at your weaknesses. Could you open up new opportunities by eliminating or managing your weaknesses? Threats: These are the negative external conditions that will get in your way. These are obstacles that are on the horizon that may affect your wellbeing and productivity.

Shortcut: Remember, don't personalize all this. When a man needs to lose ten pounds he can say so with complete frankness. He doesn't buy a girdle. He goes to gym and puts the fork down if he's serious.

Example: Here is an example of a SWOT analysis performed by one of our clients whose Big Dream was to get her abusive boyfriend to become her knight in shining armor. Like most beautiful and capable women she was brainwashed into a relationship with a complete douche. She's our favorite kind of client in that she is willing and ready to get honest. She was prepared to begin to embrace her inner smart girl first and to relegate her outer pretty girl to the back burner in order to make some changes. Her LCD indicated GGT's of Beauty and Energy, which we could see immediately from the get-go, so it became a question of whether or not she was accurately harnessing her abilities as incorporated into her Big Dream. She made no bones at all about soliciting feedback from her four sources which were her sister, her roommate, her college professor and her best friend. She assimilated the feedback from others along with her own into the following SWOT which helped her realize some opportunities for her modeling career that were being overshadowed by her home drama with her piece of shit boy-toy.

Strengths
Legs
Height
Brains
Education
Grit & Energy
Class & Style

Weaknesses
Tits (too small)
Face (plain Jane)
Clothes (hum drum)
Emotionally unstable
Poor emotional support from family
Showing up to work with bruises and having to cancel photo shoots

Opportunities
Fashion Week audition this month
Spread in Time Out NY this month
Chance to bond with a new agent who is young and energetic

Threats
Being unable to pay rent, expenses
Escalating Drug and Alcohol use
Abusive Boyfriend

We then take our model friend's SWOT and encourage her to expand upon her strengths and opportunities and minimize her weaknesses and threats. As with so many of our client's, our model friend will easily capitalize on her strengths and opportunities by eliminating her most serious threats (abusive boyfriend, drug and alcohol abuse, financial issues) while seeking to manage her weaknesses (emotional instability, poor familial support) by moving forward to the next step.

Gardening Tip: Get ready to cultivate yourself by listening to feedback, breaking up your surface, removing weeds, and preparing yourself for planting. The fertilizer is there and has prepared you for remarkably efficient, directed growth.

Step Five... Tending

Golly it's tempting to open up an issue of Harper's Bazaar and think about what you don't have.

Of course this perfectionism is encouraged among females- perfect body, perfect house, perfect life. Even after the advent of self-help we're still trying to convince ourselves to keep striving as if perfection were something that human effort could achieve.

These unrealistic expectations are rooted in comparison, the act of placing yourself in competition with someone else. Competition can be a toxic thing, if you let it.

Like fear, competition can be productive, if you channel it into action.

However, in writing this book and evaluating our processes with our clients, we have found fear to be paralyzing and something that reduces most women to acts of emotional, spiritual and physical hibernation. It's fight or flight for most mammals on this planet. We would argue that most women don't run or fight back due to our social constructs. *When faced with fear, most women freeze.* They quit moving forward. They hibernate and wait for someone to save them and make them whole again.

We're happy to help these women. We're happy to help you too.

This book is not written to encourage perfectionism among those of you that are in that way bent. This book is meant to offer short cuts as to the capable marketing of your being while at the same time encouraging you not to believe the reality of any of it.

Perfect hurts, it is destructive. Perfect is not attainable and it is not the goal.

Becoming self-actualized is the goal.

You are not your waist size. You are not the accomplishments of your children. You are not the growing pile of laundry on your basement floor.

The media wants us to think we need to be like those women splatter throughout the pages. We buy into the trash and suddenly, we have Flyover women that look like East Coast and West Coast women with nothing in between. Wake up ladies. We are not all alike. We are unique and Stepford is just a fictitious place in a movie. There is nothing to be gained by all of us attempting to compete for the same waist size, hairdo, "look", shape and size.

Personally, we like living in a place where a woman can be sexy in her own skin. Where a woman can feel confident about her internal and project that through her external. Where "sexy" is defined on our own damned terms and not by what the East Coast and West Coast thinks of our handbags, hairstyles and closets.

The external factors and manifestations are just that- external. What matters most is your internal process and the degree of peace and ease you have in your daily living.

Choose to look at your SWOT interacting with your Big Dream in the same way. The success of their interaction reflects the amount of energy you will need to expend to make your dream a reality.

Example One: Divorced. Mother of 2. Working in an administrative capacity for 25k a year. On bad terms with her ex who is a "cheap S.O.B." Mortgaged to the hilt in a condo that's not nearly enough room for her shoe collection and her kids' toys. Easily 40 lbs overweight. She meets with us because she can't find a guy who is "worth her time."

This chick's waiting for her handsome prince to arrive... Tall, dark & handsome with a net worth of about 5million. Oh and he needs to be athletic too so that she's "attracted" to him but at the same time he needs to enjoy rolling around with a woman who has a bit more love around the middle. **A relationship with a guy who will solve all her problems is her Big Dream**. How sweet, we say.

She'll tell us all about her most recent breakup and how that guy was bad about calling and proposing. She'll even tell us all about how he didn't want to move in to help her parent her two kids.
In short, the buckos she's been hanging out with don't resemble her handsome prince despite her fervent prayers to God Almighty. The SWOT analysis that she conducted in the step three would help to confirm this.

Her SWOT looks like this:

Strengths
High school diploma
Mother of 2 great kids
Diligent

Weaknesses
Overweight
Watch too much TV
Read magazines about other people's lives to escape
Gossip about others
Can't remember what it means to be excited about something
Unhappy terms with ex husband who doesn't pay enough child support
Obsessed with boss in sexual way who is unattainable

Opportunities
Go back to college
Sexy Mamas Of the Midwest   108
Dallas - Stapleton
Guide To Gardening Your Soul

Take classes through work

Threats
Late- onset Diabetes on maternal side of family
Approaching later life alone
Losing friends due to complaining and gossiping

We then begin to witness the interaction between the SWOT outcome and her identified Big Dream, in terms of the amount of energy that would be required to make this plant grow.

We live in a greening economy, which we believe reflects our spiritual selves' aspiration to expend energy wisely rather than frenetically.

This principle of energy conservation is the foundation of Step Five.

It is most natural to any system to do what comes easily and naturally to it, with the least amount of energy, which moves in the direction of the principal of grace. By doing what comes naturally to a system, the system can then do more of its G-D given purpose, oftentimes with superhuman strength.

In evaluating someone's interaction between their Big Dream and their SWOT analysis, we find ourselves looking for signs of ease and grace in the progression toward fulfillment. We look for indications that the individual will not have to excoriate herself in order to accomplish their goal, because excoriation hurts and is not loving to the self or others. Additionally, by directing a ton of energy at a goal, we can alienate the under-evolved parts of ourselves and others, so it becomes a question of whether or not ends (the Big Dream) justify the means (Energy Output).

We add up the totals of every item in her SWOT-
3 identified strengths
7 identified weaknesses

2 identified opportunities
3 identified threats

On the positive side of things we add together her **strengths and opportunities** (3 + 2) for a total of 5.

On the negative side of things we add together her **weaknesses and threats** (7 + 3) for a total of 10.

Our little lady's LCD is the **fraction equivalent of her opportunities (5) over her weaknesses** (10) which is 5/10. When you reduce the fraction to its lowest common denominator (LCD) you get **1/2**.

In short, our client's **deficits outweigh her attributes by 2 times** which suggests that a lot of energy would need to be directed toward building this LCD and increasing her attributes to the point where they exceed her deficits, which is the pre-requisite for accomplishing any dream.

Your G-D will not accomplish miracles for you without your help. And if your current manifestation isn't even close to the Big Dream you have, then it will remain a dream, not a reality, because it does not make sense for your G-D to accomplish.

A lot of what we do in our consulting practice is to make women aware of where they fall in the evaluation of their LCD as it relates to their Big Dream.

We will sit down with our client and present the facts (the LCD) to them. We will present their Big Dream. We will make a decision based on our expertise, a verdict on the energy output required to fulfill this girl's dream in the most basic magic eight ball terms of yes, no or maybe.

The verdict for our Well Meaning Mother of Two?

Jess & Rita: Maybe.

We wait for her response. We look closely at her emotional reaction to our words, if any. We look for signs that she is hedging. We look for signs that she is committed. How important is it?

Evaluating the amount of energy (time, energy, resources) required to accomplish her Big Dream is a no-nonsense wake up call for all of our clients. It is often illuminating as one becomes aware of the distance between what you want and what you've got to work with.

Our girl, despite her well-meaning intentions and moral fortitude may need to reevaluate her Big Dream or risk burning herself out.

Is it dysfunctional, then, for our Well-Meaning Middle Aged Mother of Two to want the 5 million dollar man?
No more than it is for our model friend in the previous chapter to want to make a reasonable man out of a sociopath.

Miracles do happen. We're here to happily endorse that reality. However, it is a question of what you want to be expending your energy on. If your Big Dream requires you to expend a massive amount of energy to get it going it might be an indication that you're overlooking your GGT's in a big bad way.

As previously stated, there is no capricious higher power out there somewhere assigning you to some sort of predestined fate. Life is not a shit box for some and a siesta for others. When you are moving in accordance with the will of your G-D (which is increased happiness and ease in your daily living) through honoring your unique GGT's, circumstances will fall into place to achieve a Big Dream that is so unbelievably suitable that your mind reels with excitement. You will become enlightened as to the direction of your highest purpose because you will be **saturated in inspiration**.

Your LCD will allow to you look at what you want (step 2) and what you've got (step 4) and get to work in step 5.

Shortcut: While our LCD status and Big Dream may be poetic and encouraging works, our SWOT analysis hardly ever is. If accurate, you will have a commanding indication of the directional flow of your energy and how much is required to accomplish your Big Dream, given your current evolution. So as with all things, simplify, simplify, simplify. And if you need a litmus test for whether you are exercising the principle of Energy Conservation which is in line with the will of your G-D you may want to examine your feeling states in every area of your life. If you are getting in line with the will of your G-D your life will feel harmonious. Your body will feel healthier. Your mind will feel clearer.

Your G-D wants you to conserve your energy because the Universe has great plans for you. If you are exhausted, your G-D cannot move through you.

Meditation: When we rush through our daily activities we lose ourselves and lose our valuable energy. When we rush through our daily activities it is a great indication that we are lacking in self love. Try saying I love you to yourself the next time you are tempted to rush or wake up in the middle of a rush-isode. Saying I love you will bring you back to your center, back to the peace of your Spiritual Self, who is unaffected by all of the hub-bub around you that they physical and emotional bodies get caught up in. You can short circuit through all the perfectionism in the world when you say to yourself: "I love you... I love you so much... There is nothing in the world that you could possibly do to disappoint me." Once again you are practicing Ho Oponopono a la Dr. Len and bringing about a great shift in consciousness in the world around you. LOVE dissolves all the rush and fear and inadequacy in the world. LOVE gives us the spaciousness to be serene, to be discerning, to toss aside emotional entanglements and be creative in our problems solving. LOVE opens us up to that critical element of the sexy mama: fearlessness.

Gardening Tip: Stop being dormant and get busy living! There is a saying, Do it now. Whatever it is. Do it. Now. There is no better time to exercise your initiative than this freakin' instant. So go. Go on. Do it! Now! (pssssst: we love you!)

Step Six... Facing the Elements

Does anyone find it attractive or endearing when a 4-year-old whines and moans to get what she wants? It is so frustrating to see the well-intentioned mother give in to the pleas and provide the child with her demands only to find out moments later that it was a temporary appeasement and the child will find something else to gripe about soon enough. While the whining stopped for a short time, she has taught her daughter that this bratty behavior will win! Fast forward 25 years and you have a helpless, pathetic woman who will expect society, a man, and a G-D to step in a rescue her with immediate gratification rather than get up off her buttinski to do something to fix her unpleasant surroundings herself. Teach yourself to fish ladies! Mothers, teach your daughters to fish!

Example: Rita grew up in the Midwest and was raised to participate in the family and to take responsibility for her self and not rely on a man to do it for her.

She is quickly passing this value system onto her 4 children ages Toddler to Teen. Rita learned early on that she would spend her days fixing problems, breaking up fights, giving into demands, providing things that children were capable of doing for themselves if she didn't strap teach her children to resolve issues for themselves.

While they are not growing up "Beaver" her 3 boys know how to make their own beds, load the dishwasher, sweep, dust, do laundry assist with all chores and most of all respect women. Rita's goal is to raise good men and have in-laws who don't blame her.

These kids are learning that mom isn't doing it all for them. As far as who is in charge? When the Toddler girl threw herself to the ground in the grocery store, Rita calmly picked her up, slung her over her shoulder like a sack of potatoes and walked out. Sensing defeat, the child uttered "I walk now". She's teaching her early on, that whining isn't going cute and won't work.

Are you following us here? We aren't telling you to go out and get a fishing license (unless, of course, that is your Big Dream). We are advocating that you make your own parade and stop complaining, stop whining and get busy fixing things for yourself and for the betterment of your emotional and physical well being.

Nobody is going to do it for you. And, you'll look silly as an adult getting carried out of a store kicking and screaming.

Yes, we know that many of you had traumatic childhoods. We both suffered our own share of abuse and we are not looking at this topic lightly. This can have lasting affects on your emotional health and we want you to stop living in the past, grab onto the bad stuff and say "You know what? You are not going to control my future".

Let's stop using past abuse, past trauma, past setbacks, past relationships, past failures, past this, and past that to determine the course of our futures. It happened, it hurt, it sucked and it was effed up. Somebody didn't take care of your emotional and physical well-being when you needed it most. Are you going to use that as an excuse now to not do that for yourself?

Only YOU can take responsibility for your well-being.

No matter what happened to you nobody stole you.

You have the ability to shape your future as you see it as a woman of substance who has been through some crapola and now has the ability to shape her character as she sees fit.

There is nothing dysfunctional about the overweight receptionist wanting to become a supermodel. It is simply a matter of the amount of willing one is willing to expend to accomplish one's Big Dream. It's completely feasible that our lil' receptionist could accomplish her

Big Dream if she aligns herself with GGT's that reflect such a manifestation and has the energy to put forth into achieving her goal.

We love the underdog in this country, especially in the Midwest. The rags to riches story of the trailer trash that pulled herself up from the grips of poverty, got an education, improved herself and is now a multi-millionaire...

Get busy believing that that you can be anything on your own steam. This is a much more realistic story than the prostitute who gets rescued by the rich businessman, ala "Pretty Woman."
Attention all ladies who believe in the "Pretty Woman propaganda"---
Wake up Please! Your knight in shining armor's horse is dead, his armor is rusted and he's traveling on foot to bang his mistress at the Budget Inn.

When you expect to be rescued from yourself you are giving others the credit for your *becoming*. Quit it. You too are a creature of your own design and ambition. You can transform any circumstance into an opportunity for still more personal evolution!!!

When you look at your LCD status and compare what you have to your Big Dream what's in between?

Is your lack of becoming attributed to creative reasoning?

Is it realistic to pursue your Big Dream while attending to your worldly obligations at the same time (going to work, taking care of kids, etc.)?

Absolutely.

It is simply a matter of timing. It is simply a question of when you are ready to be fully alive, a quality that every *responsibility* of yours will categorically benefit from.

Your dreams can recover from anything. Literally. Because you are in the process of living, opening, and accepting your GGT's.

When you are living someone else's dreams you are slowly closing down around your own pain. You are denying yourself the opportunity to be you.

Example: If a man gets on the scale and realizes he needs to lose 20 pounds, he will not cry and moan about it. He will not try to hide it by buying a bigger size. He will not starve himself for a few days and then step back on the scale, see a 2 pound loss and then eat like shit again because he deserves it (after all, he just lost 2 pounds). The dude will get off his ass and go to the gym OR he will accept the 20 pounds because he knows he has 20 other appealing attributes.

When an unmotivated woman realizes she needs to lose 20 pounds (she knew she needed to lose 5, and then 10, and then 15 and then it got to 20), she will immediately become down on herself and get depressed. She will get on the scale naked just to see if the number will come down a little. She will try to justify that it her "period" is coming. Anything to make herself feel better about the fact that she just ate her way to 20 extra pounds. She will talk for several days, possibly weeks about how she "needs to diet", all the while plowing through her meals like a pig in a trough. Why isn't this woman making provisions for her physical health? Why is she making excuses for herself? Why isn't she getting up off her ass and doing something about the 20 pounds? Change the behavior that got you there in the first place. It is nobody else's fault. Nobody held you down and put the cookie in your mouth. Nobody locked the door to the gym.

Exercise: What is your biggest issue that is getting in the way of accomplishing your dreams? What is holding you back from being the greatest manifestation of self? If u were writing your novel starring you how would the story progress? If you were giving an interview today on the course of your Big Dream and the obstacles you overcame what would it sound like?

If we looked at our Model Friend's example from Step Four (the girl who was trying to get her abusive boyfriend to turn into a human being), we'd begin this step by laying out the tools from the previous steps in front of her. We'd show her in black and white her GGT's, her Big Dream, her LCD & SWOT analysis and then we'd ask her to determine the true directional flow of her life's purpose. We'd pull out the math on her and give her the breakdown on how she's currently spending her energy. We'd look for her reactions, her indications of how important the realization of her dream was. It's pretty evident to us that her G-D was urging her to pursue a successful modeling career, not a psychic makeover of a sociopath. We'd illuminate her as to the abundance of opportunities and strengths that speak to this path, evidenced by the LCD fraction. We would also advise her of the value of a period of abstinence from emotional entanglements with the opposite sex until she achieved the financial success and strength of character required for her to address the issues that have led to her to find abusers attractive and make another choice.

If we looked at our Well-Meaning Mother of Two's SWOT and LCD status to approach this step we'd encourage her to also begin to validate the directional flow of her life's purpose- which was to find something to get passionate about other than magazines and romance novels. We'd encourage her to discover some of her opportunities that point toward a more creative path now that her kids are school aged and she has the chance to spend more time discovering who she truly is- which if we were to venture a guess is something along the lines of a potential novelist or musician. We would actually encourage our Well-Meaning Mother of Two to dream a Bigger Dream and return to Step 2 as we would wager that even with access to the Five Million Dollar Man she wouldn't have the tools to keep him as she simply lacks a sense of worldliness. She's about as deep as a swimming pool at present but if she were to pursue her GGT's we think all of that she would gain access to her G-D's insights and get ridiculously sexy.

Example: We love Oprah and we'll tell you why. When she started out she was thin and now she's not. She's vacillated between extremes in weight gain all the while managing to amass a fortune of Carnegie proportions. No bad for a girl from the "wrong side of the tracks." However, the public loves to follow her weight fluctuations as if her bodily image were an accurate reflection of the quality of woman that she is. Oprah is a wonderful validator of one of our key markers- "the how important is it" concept.

Research tells us that if you're fat- you will make less money. For Oprah, her weight just isn't that important, otherwise she'd be a freak of anorexic proportions considering the crowd she runs with (movie stars, sports moguls, generally individuals for whom their outsides are more important than their insides). For Oprah, she has a quality of life that she'd like to protect. She enjoys food. She enjoys rest. She enjoys working out but not at a freakish level. She has elected not to have children, not to be married, not to weigh 90 pounds and we'd say, judging by her current life that she's figured out what makes her tick as evidenced by her enormous wealth and positive effect on millions of people. Oprah didn't have to be perfect as she was breaking through the glass ceiling. She said "eff it" to all that and made her own rules. Start making your own and when you do, just watch the inspiration ripple right off you to others.

Meditation: Oftentimes, our "inner critic" limits our potential to achieve our GGT's. Our inner critic can be the internalized opinions of others that mask our true gifts and truest LCD. If you have a bad case of the internal saboteur, we advise you seek the help of a trained mental health therapist to address those negative cognitions. Tracking your thoughts with a trained other is another path to the soul and can increase your speed to Sexy Mama-dom.

Gardening Tip: Don't become root-bound. Your roots will become tangled together and stunt your growth. Dream big and "re-pot" yourself so you can grow upward and outward.

Step Seven... Sustainable Growth

"The theys" did a study with Harvard MBA grads in the 80's wherein each was asked to identify where they would be in 5 years. The ones who were precise (2%) and clearly stated their goals actually attained them. The ones who painted an overall picture (10%) achieved some success in their identified areas. The ones who were broad stroke painters (78%) did jack. Our point: Get precise about what you want.

The Universe loves specificity. Visualize what your results look like and refer to them daily.

This is a process of goal planning, reevaluation and increasing specificity, as you get closer to the mark.

The Universe is calling you to be your perfect realization of self. Goals will keep your focused on the process of "becoming".

Inertia, apathy and negative beliefs allow your life to pass you by. We as human beings so often vacillate between justifying our laziness with rational acceptance: I like who I am at present ("I'm good enough, I'm smart enough...") and secretly hating ourselves and our lack of perfection ("Golly my thighs are fat so I am a piece of excrement...").

When you see something that you want does it motivate you, or do you compare? Do you think of all the reasons to tear down the other person? Are you a woman who doesn't want to be friends with other pretty women? With prettier women? If she's thin, she must be starving. If she got the job she must've slept with someone....blah blah blah... Could it just be that she's smart, healthy and in a great relationship?

When you insult others you're advertising that you've lost your spiritual connection. You're declaring your dysfunction to your G-D

Sexy Mamas Of the Midwest   120
Dallas - Stapleton
Guide To Gardening Your Soul

and to the world. You're justifying your laziness with hate. In the words of Stephen Covey- make your own weather and carry it with you.

What are you going to spend that energy on - sitting on the couch, watching television and eating some high caloric processed poop? What a bastardization of effing potential!
Go ahead and get down and dirty with your bad self. Get so honest it motivates you into action. If you want to be thinner, go do it! If you want to be a millionaire do it. Just do it, stop talking about it!

Yack, yack, yack that's all women do according to men, right? If you believe popular myth, women are all talk, no action. We say bullshit. We say we're so much more than that. Yes, we love to talk about stuff, but we are also capable of moving into action.

We can't impart to you the number of conversations we've had with women who have an "almost dream" story. It's emotionally exhausting for us and quite troubling. Women in the Midwest and Flyover states have brilliance, potential and all the tools necessary to take on the world and are sometimes trapped in a sense of honor and duty. It is time ladies to find a balance between that honor and fulfilling our dreams.

Our discussions give us the motivation to get things done where our society might say no way Joselita!

Please understand that it takes a tremendous amount of focus to accomplish your goals. It takes so much momentum!

For some, the momentum is lacking due to a need to refocus on ourselves. You aren't doing fat, lazy, lying activities. On the contrary, you are spread to thin. Your dreams aren't even on the horizon. Perhaps you are the president of the PTA, the coach of your daughter's soccer team, organizer for the neighbor parties, working part-time/full-time, married or single mom, and on and on. You just haven't found the time to chase your dreams because you are on the doorstep of everyone else's.

Now, If all you're doing is fat, lazy, lying activities, what substance can a man derive from you? Just your vagina. You don't have anything interesting to discuss because you're not becoming worldly. You're unappealing physically because you're doing fat activities. You've got nothing spiritual or moral going on because you're not involved in any sort of greater quest. You are just a wide open vagina wafting in the breeze.

And since you're so hell bent on marketing your vagina instead of other aspects of your being he's going to take a snatch of that vagina and be confused by your level of offense when he takes off. It's like changing the rules of baseball and saying, "You must do a cartwheel after you cross home plate". A man is going to say, "Wait a second, you can't change the rules! I already crossed home plate!" Don't get offended when you're not playing according to the rules. Don't think for a minute that you can lead with your vagina and then pull a switcheroo in your marketing. Talk about false advertising!

You tell us that you're exhausted by life, but how much energy are you wasting on fat, lazy activities and lying activities to justify your lack of movement toward your true goals?

Flyover women especially have way too much potential to spend it not achieving their goals. You are managing families, the PTA, are working moms, volunteers in your communities. What you need to be conscience of is that you don't ignore your own dreams along the way.

Where are you? Where are you going? How are you going to get there? These seem like such simple questions if the answers are "I'm standing here, I'm going to the store and I'm driving a car." But, how many of you can answer these questions if you know that we are talking about your personal goals?

Exercise One: So where are you, truly? Have you taken the time to assess yourself? Do you like where you are in terms of education, health, relationships, career, community, financials, family, faith, etc? Is there something missing? A lot missing? What does it feel like, today, to be you? How does it feel to wake up in your skin each day? Can you face yourself in the mirror and say "I like how I look, how I feel, what I am doing, who I am doing it with/for, and what I've become?" Are you fulfilled and living up to your potential? Our guess is you wouldn't be reading this book if you felt really good about these first questions.

So…How are you going to get achieve your Big Dream? How will you shift your LCD in order to achieve your goals? What do you need to do? A means of shifting your LCD toward your identified dream are the ways in which we build our portfolio as entrepreneurs. Let's dive in right now…

10, 9, 8, 7, 6, 5, 4, 3, 2, 1……"HAPPY NEW YEAR!!!

We all join in this familiar tradition on the eve of every December 31st and the next morning the ritual continues as many well-intended ladies declare their Resolutions! Ahhhh… a RESOLUTION. It sounds so official and noble. Of course you will stick to it; after all, you declared it!

Let's get real here. Why do you think that gym memberships go up a gazillion percent in January and yet attendance at the gym seems to wane by mid February?

Because we are liars! We lie to make ourselves feel better cuz our parents said so or society said it was best, but if we're not following through with it how are we creating more joy and peace for ourselves?

Oh, I'm going to start working out 3 days per week. I'm going to put away more money in savings. I'm going to go back to school. I'm going to (insert bullshit resolution here). Why don't folks stick with their resolutions? Cuz they're not real goals. They're bullshit that they feel they need to do, otherwise they would have made them a reality.

There are entire industries built upon perpetuating your guilt about what a crappy person you think you are (if you still believe this, refer back to Step 1).

Stop buying the effing product, doll faces, if you don't believe in the goal! Start marketing your own product, your own beliefs that accurately reflect the person you believe yourself to fundamentally be!

Real goals have a plan. Without a plan, your goal is just sitting out there in a perpetual wasteland untouched and unrealized...

Who owns the plan for your life's goals? Your boyfriend? Neighbor? Boss? Parents? Husband? Wrong! You own it. If you set a goal, then it is not really going to come to fruition until there is a plan.... Period.

"The Theys" suggest several ways to approach setting your goals. Some say you sit down and develop goals based on specific categories. Others say that can bog you down with too many goals to attain and you should limit yourself to setting a "5 year plan".
Exercise Two: In our experience, the best way to set your personal goals is to just sit down with a clean sheet of paper and do a brain dump. See where your mind storms. Picture, as we mentioned above, the "ideal you". What does "she" look like? What does she have? What does she do? Who is in her life? What surrounds her? How does she behave? How does she feel?

There is tremendous power in writing it down. The old business saying is "get it in writing" and this is no different than having a contract with yourself.

Your "Reach for the Sky" step can help to solidify this. Look at your goals.

You may have written "travel", or "own a house". Perhaps you wrote "exercise more" or "have children".

Good starting points, but in order to be well-defined goals, we will ask that you use the following principle to develop your goals. We are asking you to get PLANT on your goals and get them working for you. What is PLANT you ask?
Ahem...

A goal isn't well defined in our minds unless it is a **PLANT.**

P – Precise

L – Level – Headed

A – Achievable

N – Numerable

T – Timely

PLANT goals are specific and cut the emotionality out of everything. They are clear and achievable.

There is a saying we use in business, the 5Ws and 1H (Where, When, Who, Why, How) that can help you develop your PLANT goal statement for each target weakness and threat. When you PLANT solutions in your SWOT analysis, specifically your weaknesses and threats, you minimize their effects on your LCD until you get to a place where they're no longer factored into the equation. You get to a place where your LCD indicates that your strengths are outweighing your deficits.
Example: Here's an example of a PLANT analysis on *fitness* that we did with our Well Meaning Mother of Two...
Reach high brainstorm: Being fit
What will accomplish this? Exercise

Sexy Mamas Of the Midwest   125
Dallas - Stapleton
Guide To Gardening Your Soul

Where will I accomplish this? Buff-bodies gym
When will I accomplish this? 3 times per week for 30 minutes each right after work
Who will I accomplish this with? Alone
Why is this important to me? Because I want to be healthy and look better, feel better and fit into some hot clothes
How will I accomplish this? I will do a combination of cardio and resistance training
PLANT Goal Statement: I will exercise 3 times per week for 30 minutes each right after work at buff bodies gym

Shortcut: Make sure you make your PLANTs numerable and achievable as you begin to problem solve. If you know that your schedule doesn't allow for you to ever go to the gym 3 days per week right after work, then don't set that as a goal or you are already failing. Instead, perhaps set up a weekend training plan. And by the way, if you can't find time to exercise, you'd better look at your schedule and figure out why you can't. What "fat" activities are you doing? Remember, any activity you are doing that keeps you fat or while you are fat is a "FAT" activity. If you are working out, these are your "getting into shape" activities

Warning: Be careful of making non-numerable goals. When we identify a goal that is: "drink less coffee," that is not numerable so there is less accountability to self. If you reframe your goal into numerable terms it would look something like this: I will limit my daily coffee intake to one 6oz serving per day and only before 12:00 p.m. Now that, darlings, is numerable.

The Plan

Once you have defined all of your goals, you will need a plan to reach them. Think of it like going on a vacation. You're going on this great trip to the Bahamas (your goal).

How are you going to get there? I'm sure you managed to get a plane ticket or other means of transportation. You didn't just expect to beam yourself to the beach, did you?

What will go in your suitcase? These are the little things that you will need once you reach your destination. Be prepared. You'll need your awesome bikini, flip flops, sunscreen, floppy hat, trash mags, etc. You don't want to show up in the Bahamas with your snow boots and skis! Everyone would question why you wanted to be there in the first place.

Did you need to prepare things before you left? Hold the mail? Make arrangements for your pets? (If you have more than 2 cats, perhaps you need this book more than you thought!) Do you need a good waxing? You wouldn't go on a trip without taking care of these details.

We're talking about a plan here, ladies.

How does the saying go? "Prior proper planning prevents piss poor performance"

Let's not piss your goals down a toilet. If you want to reach your goals, you must plan to reach your goals. It will not happen just because you WILL it to happen.

Women come to us so often to tell us about weight, their poor health, their uninspiring careers, their misguided relationships, their financial situations. We continue to tell them the same thing we are telling you. Only YOU can direct the course of your present state and your future.

If you want to do something about it and want to change the course of your life, then take action instead of taking another bite of cheesecake! Set PLANT Goals and reach them and in no time you will become the Sexy Mama you were meant to be!

Gardening Tip: While dormancy works for plants, this is not what you are looking for in life. You don't need a yearly cycle where your growth slows and you rest. Get moving on your goals

Step Eight... Beautifying Your Surroundings

Unless you are completely psychotic 100% of the time you possess insight into your character. You know when you have effed up. You carry that with you, that guilt, and it continues to color your present. That's why we do service, because it allows us to create new beliefs about ourselves. We aren't so very selfish if we are putting others' needs before our own.

Why do we serve?

- We serve so that we can think better of ourselves and be reminded of our fundamental goodness.
- We serve so that we can demonstrate through action- as proof to ourselves (our worst critics) that we are perhaps better off than we originally thought- perhaps better than Mom or Dad said we were.
- We can serve others so we do not engage in our own stuff full time.
- We serve others so that we do not engage in flattery of self or others.
- We serve to get a more accurate reflection of our truest nature

We are loved by our G-D and in serving (loving our fellow as little more) we grow in closeness to our higher power, who is the greatest source of healing.

How do we serve?

- By volunteering for a local nonprofit.
- By contributing to a cause that we believe in.

- By sharing our story with others and inspiring the less motivated among us.
- By engaging in simple activities like baking cookies for a new neighbor and not expecting anything in return.
- By doing something kind and not telling anyone about it.
- Through any action which decreases the distance between our G-D and us.

What does an act of service do?

- Keeps us busy.
- Dissipates our fear of daily living and gets us actively involved in problem solving for the greater good.
- Serving gives us magnetism and an air of productivity.

There is a natural magnetism that develops when fear begins to remove itself from your life. There is a natural magnetism that develops when you know that you are genuinely bettering the planet. When you understand where you end and others begin yet still make efforts to bridge gaps in understanding.

The Magnetic Woman is the Great Woman we previously discussed. She is, truly, a rare and magnificent thing.

The Magnetic Woman has let go of all of the hot air. She has had her dark night of the soul, has stared it down, and has chosen to keep living. She may have momentary annoyances throughout her day but she knows how to process her frustrations and let go of the bullshit. She knows how to allow pain to carve out a bit more space within her for her Divine Purpose to get through. She knows that pain will come but suffering is optional. She is in charge.

The Magnetic Woman is the Great Woman who is attached to worldly things insofar as they will serve her in her evolution toward LOVE. The Magnetic Woman develops more fully in relationship with others like her, who support her, who embody their own process of moving toward LOVE. The Magnetic Woman has a Magnetic Man who is her spiritual equal and who accompanies her on a similar journey toward still more love and flexibility.

Women who are raised in Middle America know all too well the importance of this step. We are raised to value the beautification of our surroundings. From the time we are old enough to "get it", we are encouraged to join clubs and organizations that raise money for our communities. We share our time and talents so that others less fortunate may grow. This is something we do without much thought. We dig deep in our pockets and if we don't have the cash, we give our time. It is hard for us to say no.

Example: Both of us tithe and contribute regularly to nonprofits that we believe in. Regardless of the amount of money we have made or have not made, according to the changing financial times, we endeavor to contribute 10% of our income annually. We estimate that we give enough to feel a slight pinch in order to feel that we are contributing to the solution in social arenas rather than the problem. So we go without that new car this year, so what. We're helping young children have access to healthy lunches, contributing household items to domestic violence shelters and sharing our financial blessings with our local homeless shelter. Why do we do it? Because it makes us feel really good and feeling good daily is our goal.

Gardening Tip: Just as many plants are not as hardy under certain conditions, you must learn to acclimate yourself to new scenarios, learn tolerance and move outside your protected areas

Step Nine... Community

We were sitting in our local coffee shop recently trying to clear our heads.

We look forward to these peaceful moments, away from the chaos of households full of children and the responsibilities that naturally come with them. While we love our families and all that being mothers, wives, and daughters entails, we find that if we don't refuel our souls regularly that we will not be as productive in those roles.

So we do the "we" time which is our version of "me" time but in one another's company to encourage our continued growth. We've found that when you have a friend as a witness it helps to encourage your individual growth because you're supported. We often sit side by side doing "our own thing" and then touch base to get feedback.

However, inspiration comes in the unlikeliest of places, we've found.

So we're in the coffee shop. We were positioned in our favorite spots- near the window in the comfy chairs. Armed with our favorite doses of caffeine, we sat down to write another chapter of this book. The birds could be heard singing a familiar tune and the sun was beaming through the windows. We were at peace.

Suddenly...

A shrill, piercing cry shatters the morning quietude. The hairs on Rita's arms stood to attention as this unpleasant clatter continued. Jessica's stomach gurgled expectantly for her coffee but was unrewarded as she lost the grip on her cup.

Who dared interrupt our peaceful, serene moment?

The thems. That's who. You know the type.
A gaggle of grouchy, grumpy, crabby 30-plus-year-old women who were bellyaching and whining about their bleak and meaningless existences.

Very attractive and very sexy, wouldn't you say?

What were they grousing about? You name it.

 It was nothing of substance.

- We just got back from vacation and the waiter at the one restaurant was so rude, you wouldn't believe it! (You just had a vacation, lady!)
- I am totally the one who keeps this relationship together. He has no appreciation for me!
- I just bought this purse and it is driving me nuts. The handle is too short.
- Can you believe they were out of whipped cream? My drink is ruined!
- I am so sick of my job, I should totally quit!
- This diet I am on produces zero results!
- He is so annoying and he thinks he is so cool, what a moron!
- I have so much to do. I'm the room mom for school and it is just way too much work!
- My period started!

Our favorite. Acquired community as the direct result of complaining. Ugh…

It is our firm belief that there is something gorgeous in each and every one of us and that once harnessed, this energy and uniqueness can be used to encourage development in the parts that are yet undiscovered or not quite as wonderful as we would like them to be.

Dallas - Stapleton
Guide To Gardening Your Soul

Believe this.

Surround yourself with people who believe this.

Hiding amongst nasty bitchy little morons just makes you a nasty bitchy little moron.

Please, doll-faces... Have a clue how to have a conversation with other folks that is *uplifting and independent of bellyaching.* When you spread chronic negativity it infects others as well as yourself! How are you to become a sexy mama when you're so busy filtering and adding to the shit storm?

Ladies, please! We as a species need to cease acting as if we are merely pawns in the game of life!

The Flyover states can be the first to start this movement and quit with the griping and get busy with *becoming something.*

You can choose how you approach things in your life and the perceptions you have. Challenge your assumptions about the way things are and the way you want them to be. Put yourself in charge and stop whining and complaining about all the things that went "wrong" or could go "wrong" and start believing in and focusing on all the things that went "right" or will go "your way."

Negativity is the thief of joy. It is a contagion that feeds upon the weak and uninspired among us.

Our solution? Get inspired about something.

Exercise: Scientists believe it takes 21 days to form a new habit. Our challenge to you is this. Spend the next 21 days getting inspired about

21 different things. In doing so you will successfully remove all whining, bitching, gossiping and complaining from your existence. It will be tough, but we believe you can do it. Pick up a book that completely transports you, take up running, go to a museum, play guitar hero with your kids… Some sort of daily activity that allows you to reboot the computer as it were. An activity that allows you to wipe yourself clean of the days events and responsibilities in preparation for what will arrive shortly… Your authentic self.

The authentic self does not speak to the person who's too busy bitching to live in the moment. The authentic self does not speak when there's an overabundance of responsibility that freezes us in what many would consider to be an *adult* mentality but is actually martyr mode as we like to call it. The authentic self comes when there is abundant joy and satisfaction in your heart and in your head. It breaks through when we have gratitude for the good and the bad in our lives and still know how to face the day with the deep belief that things can and will be okay. Authenticity radiates faith in something greater than yourself, be it love, beauty, humanism or something akin to G-D.

Authenticity is just as contagious as negativity.

How many times do we feel drawn to the woman who may not have the biggest checking account in the world but who radiates peace and ease in her daily existence? This woman has identified her primary goal and is living it and hasn't circumnavigated *the work of life* which quite simply is self actualization.

It is our contention that we are searching for this same peace and ease in our lives when we go after external fixes to fill the internal hole in the form of food, sex, ambition, etc. These quick fixes as we like to call them only fill the hole inside us for a short time before we are faced with the bleak nothingness or the dark night of the soul.

Believe in something wonderful, ladies. Believe even when everyone else does not. Surround yourself with positive reflections of your belief that everything will be okay.

And when you run out of steam, safeguard your becoming by surrounding yourself with likeminded individuals who are working just as diligently on themselves!

Exercise Two: Find yourself some cool chicks who are moving toward their goals, who are interested in outgrowing their current frame of reference. Uplift one another. Establish a community of women with like ideals. Find women who are reading this book, who are delving into what it means to be authentically them. Find individuals to surround yourself with who are on spiritual quests, who are hungering after something intangible, who are in the world being challenged, refusing to sit high on a mountain top looking down upon others. Join our website and find a unique community of women who are willing to impart their own brand of wisdom, informed by their decision to take life as life comes while at the same time remaining hopeful. Form a Sexy Mama study group in your home town to spread the message of inspiration to women of all ages and stages of life!

We are all parts of the same woman. The difference between us is our reflected happiness. You can look at a woman's poor self-image and gather that is the result of a negative experience that she has yet to learn from. You can look at another woman's acquired confidence and surmise that it is the result of increasing confidence in her ability to provide for herself and her loved others. We can identify and learn from each other when we get together.

The Universal Language of Love allows us to navigate different discourses (feminist, radical, traditional, uneducated, youthful, sage, and academic) without seeing the differences between us. We truly are a community. We must begin to transmit LOVE to one another and dissolve divisions with forgiveness for the under-evolved aspects of ourselves that want to gripe and pick at the girl next door.

This is our Movement. It's starts with us. Let's get back to zero and start encouraging one another toward happiness. Let's start encouraging one another toward the realization of our dreams.

It is really that simple, in our minds. We as women will evolve when we get happier and are in the company of dream-pursuing happy people.

Living authentically is the quickest fix to ridding yourself of the negative hangers-on of life. The cousin who's constantly calling you for money, the best friend who can't face her alcoholism. When we're authentic we're no longer afraid of expressing our true feelings because we feel no sense of indebtedness to anyone or anything *earthly*. We get our power from another source. We begin to figure out the difference between discernment and judgment. We lessen our emotional attachment to outcomes and opinions. We can establish boundaries with individuals if they are threats to the under-developed parts of us that are still screaming for protection and love from our G-D. We can establish distance from people that have hurt us and emotional baggage from the past. We have the right to keep the under-evolved parts of us safe while forgiving what we cannot understand a little at a time.

Discernment and boundaries are the location of effective problem solving.
Imagine how much better you will feel. It is something akin to freedom we believe to sever oneself from the compulsiveness of life. Nobody, especially a man, wants to surround themselves with chronic whiners and bitchers. How great is your average martyr in bed? Martyrs are the best at setting impossible expectations. They always whine and complain and nothing will ever please them. Do your best to remove these people from your daily lives or, better yet, try to set an

example for them on how to lead a rich life full of positive energy and free from whine.

Gardening Tip: Take steps today to Go Green. Change your bad habits and learn ways to give back to the Earth. Set a good example for others in your community. We are all mothers to something lovely whether it is just our under-developed aspects of self or actual human children; we have so much in common with our beloved planet! So please, *take the time to nurture her in a big way.* Plant a garden, nurture a soul, contribute to a better tomorrow with healthy actions and ideas. Every positive thought makes a huge difference.

Step Ten... Post-Test: Your True Plant Identity

Everyone loves our analogy of gardening when it comes to tending the soul. It's simple enough to make sense and embraces the individuality of each woman we work with.

We're willing to bet, however, that if you took the plant quiz now and compared your answers to your results to your previous ones that you'd notice a slight shift in presentation.

Perhaps you're a bit closer to Self.

So go ahead, do just that. Take the plant quiz once more and take note of any differences.

Perhaps you're getting closer to your true baseline now that you've explored who you are.

Perhaps you're not the rose you thought you were. Perhaps you're more fulfilled by supporting others and are more along the lines of a lilac.

It is so true that once you know where you are coming from you know where you are headed.

Being grounded in a meditation practice and having an awareness of a G-D transforming the less under-developed aspects of your life gives you lots of energy to be truer to your innermost self.

Working through the rest of the steps and identifying some of the false beliefs that have you trapped in old patterns, particularly the false dreams that have limited you from achieving your Big Dream, you are able to recognize the role of others in shaping your life quite against what might be your most natural GGT's and accurate LCD status.

When we know our true nature we begin to accept ourselves a little more. We begin to accept our areas that need more tending, more growth, and more attention just as we are able to acknowledge all of our goodness.
Oftentimes we have been taught to believe certain things about ourselves that are actually quite inaccurate, i.e.: I'm a Taurus so I'm stubborn or I'm female so I'm a creature of whimsy.

You have the absolute ability to shape your own fate as long as you are in line with your GGT's and LCD.

You have the absolute ability to be in the most intentional and G-D given relationship imaginable once you know how deep your roots go and how high you lift up into the sky.

You can feel free to create a totem that reflects your plant essence as well as your LCD to post on your wall for reflection. Oftentimes, when we begin to externalize our most basic inner aspects in a recognizable form that we can refer to like a picture, you find your inner strength increasing in direct response to a need to protect, respect and tend to that totem.

And as you embrace and protect that totem you will be embracing yourself and the rest of the world.

Exercise: Begin to monitor how much time you spend nurturing your outer aspects, i.e.: appearance, and attempt to spend just as much time nurturing your inner aspects, i.e.: your GGT's. For example, if you spend 1 hour getting dressed in the morning and 1 hour at the gym, begin spending at least 2 hours per day respecting your GGT's in a peaceful and restorative practice, i.e.: yoga, meditation, relaxation, creative writing, supportive company, cognitive behavioral therapy, walks in the rain, etc.…

Gardening Tip: Don't be a plant that has no nutrients. Add anything positive to your soil that you need to improve your situation. Be a specimen plant and show off your special qualities. Have a continuous growing season and cultivate your soul.

Part Three: Quick-spiration

Finding Your Joy

Jessica's mom was of the "shoulder pad generation" and by this we mean that her mom went to work full time in the 1980's with 3 kids to support, chock full of Gloria Steinem and Betty Friedan. The *Shoulder Pad Brigade*, as they will be referred to henceforth, were a bunch of 1960's liberal arts educated chickadees that were filled with the expectation that it was in fact possible to "have it all." The shoulder pad brigade was expected by their forbears like Steinem to both give birth and go to work with bells on. These middle class white chicks were instructed that they needed to be alright with poorer more ethnic women raising their kids while they jogged and opted out of oppressive systems like the PTA and bake sales and Protestantism. After all, they had more important things to do like participate equally with their husbands in the business of capitalism and become mildly alcoholic.

Needless to say, some of the shoulder pad brigade had a ball like Hillary Clinton and were rewarded with institutional power and loads of cash. Some of them started their own businesses and inspired their daughters to do the same (**thank you Jess' mom**!) We thank them for breaking through the glass ceiling and giving us a heritage to move through. G-D bless you!

Some of them, however, ended up a bit withered and bitchy. Some of these more unpleasant shoulder pad constituents radiated discontent with feminism as they had experienced in the daily living outside of the ivory tower but had no viable substitute for it other than developing a bitchy sense of competition.

"Welcome to the second shift," the exhausted malcontents said, when Jessica gave birth to her son. Motherhood, aka the Second Shift, was regarded in the same context as Aunt Flo, a thing to be endured. The expectation was that Jessica would martyr herself by working all day

Sexy Mamas Of the Midwest   143
Dallas - Stapleton
Guide To Gardening Your Soul

at her actual job and then all night at home with the kid while her husband gradually lost interest in her and ran away with his admin assistant thereby perpetuating another generation of exhausted malcontents with no reasonable substitute for the "have it all" propaganda. The shoulder padders waited in joyful hope for the coming of Jessica's martyrdom and when it didn't happen after the first kid they grew impatient. "Why hasn't she cracked up yet," they said. Herein lies the difference, Jessica said... I don't want to be exhausted anymore. There's simply no need. If I am responsible for the course of my life, I'd rather choose happiness. Eff martyrdom.

It was Jessica's contention that being perceived as inexhaustibly perfect by her peers wasn't of supreme importance, but rather, that happiness was. To Jessica, happiness involved spending more time with her son and less time at the office. Happiness involved getting the boob job she wanted one and taking her husband to a strip club because it turned him on. To Jessica, happiness was a process of constant revelation, not something to be arrived at under the auspice of career and avid social climbing.

At present, to both of us, happiness is an inside job and is not something that we can define for you, in simple terms.

We are quite sure, however, that happiness involves the conservation of energy and that it is quite impossible to tear down everything around you and rebuild successfully in one lifetime. Why throw the baby out with the bathwater, we ask. Why not build upon what exists, in an informed and interested manner. Why not have fun a little, after all happiness isn't something that arrests itself once we begin menstruating and have the mantle of womanhood thrust among us.

Let's stop being martyrs. Let's stop being warhorses. It's so dull and unfeminine.

Mean spirited folks love to put down the pretty, sweet girls. What the hell, may we ask, is so *wrong* with being perceived as "pretty" or "kind?" Kindness and appreciation for beauty are G-D given and so immensely powerful! Happiness empowers!

We say that it's empowered to get the boob job if it makes you feel sexier naked. We are, above all, proponents for living authentically.

We think that it's more valuable to be honest if it means we're happier as human beings. Life is so easy. How empowered is it to spend your days working at a job you hate? How empowered is it to have sex with someone that you're not attracted to?
There is no easy answer to all the world's ills that we've come up with thus far other than it is perhaps more important than ever to do things that perpetuate happiness. Please darlings, take the time to find your joy, whatever that is.

Example: We love Kelly Ripa and we'll tell you why. First of all, she's absolutely adorable, she's happily married and she's given birth a few times. We love that she's committed to her career and her partner but still finds time to take care of herself. Most of all we love her because she radiates spontaneity that comes as a natural byproduct of living authentically. She's not laboring under the delusion that perfection is something to be achieved. The girl admittedly works as little as possible to spend more time with her family because that is the most important thing to her. By being closer to her G-D, which is her family, she is able to embody and transmit increasing amounts of joy. That girl is happy and she's opposite Regis Philbin every day. Talk about leading a spiritual existence!

In direct contrast, let's take a look at Kathy Lee Gifford. She makes us a bit sick, honestly. She reminds us of that girl on the Homecoming Court in High School that smiled so much she had to get chemical fillers at age 17. Poor Kathy Lee. We knew the breakdown was coming when she eagerly thrust her kids upon us at every opportunity. How many Christmas Specials can one family sustain with grace? When Frank dallied elsewhere it didn't shock us at all. Men don't like perfection. Especially when it's frigid. Who cares how perfect she thinks she is. Gag us.

In short, inspiration follows joy, so find your joy, ladies. There is something honorable about the Flyover woman and we want you to live to the fullest joy you can find.

It is so much easier to write that novel you've always wanted to write or to put down all of the toxic substances you've been imbibing when you're legitimately happy. And the thing with happiness is that it is contagious. You get a little bit of it going and suddenly that little bit blossoms into even more in new areas of your life. You start a bit on that garden you've always wanted to plant and soon the resultant joy you experience from enjoying and being grateful for that garden brings you into better alignment with your perfect realization of self. Suddenly what started out as a little garden produces a better job for you, a better mate if you need one, improved relationships with the difficult people in your life.

This is our movement.

When you are able to experience more joy in your daily living you are pursuing the spiritual path and the universe will reward you with more good things to be grateful for.

Homework: Sometimes the things that you envision yourself having are just *stuff* anyway. They're not things that you legitimately want anyway so you're conflicted and perhaps that's why you haven't manifested them yet. Perhaps there's old stuff built up in your heart and your head that you need to part with and make a clean break from. Perhaps you don't have a true desire for the biggest house in the world but would rather spend your time working in a homeless shelter…

Perhaps you need to return to Step 4 and get in line, dah-leeng.

Beyond Competition

As you move closer to your goal and start to realize some of your target areas, you may notice people places and things being drawn more and more to you without any effort on your part.

This is because you are moving with the universe, not against it. You are moving toward fruition as an individual which helps the realization of the good of all beings. You are, in effect, assisting the universe in its goal, which is perfection.

Bear this in mind.

At times you may be convinced that your accomplishments are tenuous and meant for others. You may be tempted to get competitive with other folks who are performing equally or are perhaps your "betters," at this moment in time. The media will try to shove images at you that convince you to live a different way.

Do not be so dissuaded.

No one has a leg up on anyone in this world. The concept of competition is one of the greatest fallacies our time.

"Great is the man," Emerson said, "who sees that the real and true substance in this world is spiritual and not material."

Our man isn't saying this because he is on some sort of spiritual plane and has no need for material products.

He said it because our thoughts are what rule our existence, not the appearance of things.

There is another truism that is oft repeated, "that which you resist, persists." If you allow fear of losing something to dictate your life, you will lose that thing most certainly. How often do we see this demonstrated in our daily lives? Folks who work for years to amass an incredible fortune who then lose it overnight.

Plus being a competitive bitch is so un-fun. How does being a bitch add to the spirit of true wealth and progress? Isn't bitchiness merely a byproduct of believing there's not enough to go around?

When a woman is bitchy and competitive with us we merely regard the situation dispassionately and say

"Gosh that must be a drag for her. How un-fun. How NOT sexy."

Through the act of figuring out who we are as individuals we've acquired a sense of *rational attachment*. This rational attachment allows us to move through life without folks pressing our buttons. Especially folks who don't know anything about us on a personal level other than what we look like.

Add to the spirit of plenty by perpetuating more goodness, more grace, more understanding. Fear can be so unproductive. When we relax and peacefully face our fears, we emerge with confidence and courage. Too often we want to grab the pen from our G-D and write the story of our tomorrows for fear of where it is going. Remember, you are depriving yourself of your G-D's potential to spontaneously heal you when you reach for the pen and try to beat your G-D to the punch. Allow yourself to benefit from the x-factor of your G-D, your G-D's unlimited capacity for healing, balance, peace and beauty. Let your G-D write the story of you which has been there all along and has simply been covered up with *stuff.*

DO IT NOW.

Homework: The next time you see bounty evidenced around you in the form of beauty or intelligence or material substance, thank G-D for it. There is plenty to go around.

The Crazy Debate

And then, of course, there is the great crazy debate, as we like to call it.

How often do we encounter folks who project their neuroses onto those around them?

We've all had the experience of calling a former friend a "psycho." However, what does that say about us?

How are we projecting?

Perhaps we're a little bit nuts too? Perhaps we haven't softened and forgiven ourselves for our imperfections and emotionality and therefore thrust that wounded-ness upon others?

We have found that when you are confident of who you are in your heart and your head then you do not live in fear of others. You don't thrust your opinions upon them with much veracity. You exercise restraint of pen and tongue and defer judgment until more is revealed.

Oh my, that's a tough one, you say.

Well, of course, darlings. This is about growth, isn't it?

So what's the point of deferring judgment and exercising restraint in opposition to fear?

You become more confident. You spend more time working on becoming uniquely you and less time focused on the "crazies" around you. You become less fearful of repeating old stuff- acts of victimization, abuse, neglect and more concerned with the process of living in a body and mind that is capable of living. We aren't capable of living when we engage in fat, lazy and lying activities, would you agree?

Therefore, how are we capable of living fully when we are competitively focused on the activities of those around us?

We find it less oppressive to live in the Midwest because we feel less compelled to compete with one another and instead feel a bond as females.

We ask that you live life as if you are fully capable of defending yourself physically and mentally but at the same time choose to refrain from doing so out of respect for what is underdeveloped (crazy/evil) around you. Remember, not everyone has gone through the process of growing and we can only hope that one day they will.

The realization that growth needs to occur is a tough one. It is difficult to accept and some folks you encounter may never get there. But don't worry, you have a G-D who will take care of you. Your G-D gives you amazing reservoirs of strength to grow increasingly capable.

You will not be permanently maimed by anyone or anything, we promise you.

When you are confident about your ability to defend yourself with a strong warrior's body that has refrained from the FLL activities and an internal softness that is capable of forgiving and letting go of anger, then you do not live in a state of hyper arousal, always expecting something terrible to befall you.

You cease being paranoid. You acknowledge that this is, indeed, a beautiful place to exist, this planet, this country, this body, this brain, the soul.

You see that you are so much more than you thought and therefore how could you ever steep yourself in the busy-ness of judgment?

What is paranoia? Quite simply, fear of self. All of us possess the requisite good qualities and the requisite bad qualities. You don't need to go outside of yourself to understand atrocity as well as profound joy.

Paranoia is a thief. It robs you of truth. It is so easy to get caught and allow paranoia to seep into our souls and cloud our minds with "what ifs" and let fears take over all the progress made in becoming authentic. Fight the urge.

Fear is inevitable. It will come. But you don't have to be consumed by it.

If you've gone through our steps, then you are on the way to "becoming" and you will feel the fear leave you and be replaced with calm confidence in your Authentic Self. You are Becoming a Strong Sexy Mama.

G-D bless!

Wounds

Show us a woman who won't claim her wounds and we'll show you a liar.

And you know us, we don't like Lying Activities.

It is impossible to move through life and not be affected by it. Life renders you flexible, or else.

As women we know that things change. We gain and lose weight, we have babies, we crave different foods depending on the day...
There's very little permanence in our lives, blame it on having a period and surrendering our bodies to the moon once a month. This makes us different from men. It makes us more brave, and we wouldn't have it any other way.

True bravery involves the capable digesting of one's experience. True bravery doesn't deny past mistakes but sees everything as a growth experience, as an opportunity for still more spiritual development. Bravery has everything to do with turning into one's own pain and knowing that the transformation of sustaining life while actively experiencing doubt is the greatest demonstration of faith. A warrior goes into battle with open eyes to what may happen with questions still unresolved in her heart while at the same time knowing herself capable of handling whatever may arise with G-D's help.

You can be mighty because mighty forces will come to your aid.

All of the darkness is so important because it carves out space within us without our consent. After all, who would choose to encounter pain, even if it is ultimately transformative? When we experience life as life is, with all of its complications we emerge changed, a bit broken, if you will but then we are able to CHOOSE what kind of person we'd like to become as we heal instead of foreclosing upon some sort of predestined existence and in choice there is freedom.

G-D loves you and wants to transform your world. G-D wants to live in concert with you, helping you to manifest higher and higher levels of consciousness, wealth, expression, creativity, awareness, love.

It is only by revisiting our past fully with open eyes and hearts and minds that we begin to unlearn the things we've been taught to foreclose upon. That we are empowered to choose what works best for us, independent of all programming.

No matter what happened to you, you are better for having experienced it. That is a profound concept to accept and much easier to state than to live; however, we have both had to walk this walk many times and have emerged victorious.

No matter what anyone did to you, nobody stole you. You are an eternal being. You are part of the alpha and the omega. *You are stardust and tree roots and baby's tears.* You are part of the whole deal. And the more that you can rest still in that awareness, the more change you can affect upon the world.

Turn into your own pain and emerge victorious. Life will continue to happen, some good some bad, most of it just is. Continue to process and grow and evolve as you are supposed to. You have great work to do. You are already doing most of it. Find your supply and wake the eff up. YOU ARE ENOUGH.

Many of you experienced trauma or just drama in your childhood and have learned pain as a strong emotion. You have learned to feel comfort in your pain and have latched onto this emotion. How many of you are good at expressing this deep anguish inside of you?

Ladies, as adult women we need to stop using these bad coping skills as an excuse to hang onto "what was". Let's stop blaming all that went wrong, is wrong and could go wrong in our lives on our old wounds.

If not, you are stunting your sexy mama. You can't be authentic when the past is your basis for emotional reaction.

Exercise: Imagine all the wounds of your past as potatoes. Mentally place each of them in a sack. You now have to carry this sack around with you each day. Imagine this sack will get in the way of everything you do. You couldn't have crazy fun sex with your boyfriend tonight because your sack of shit is in the way. You can't get out of bed in the morning because your sack of pain was keeping you up all night. You wouldn't eat well because your sack of bull is getting in the way of you making healthy eating choices. Pretty soon this big old sack of emotional baloney is taking over your life and burlap is sooooo not your color dahling! Our advice. Set the sack aside instead. Put it away. Forget about it. Choose to live! And while you're at it... Slow down. That which you resist persists.

All of your dynamism is inside. All of your power. Like an acorn seed you possess all of the characteristics necessary to make a tree. Start looking inside. You don't need to learn a new language or travel to the other side of the world. You can do those things certainly, but the most anyone else can do is serve as a witness to your process. It is ultimately your responsibility, to sort and make sense of the mysteries inside you. To at least begin to tackle them.

That's what attracts us to folks, their bravery. The quiet one with the self assurance is the one we want for our president. The one who's fought battles of their own and become well versed in handling adversity before they take up the public mantle and do it professionally.

You are so special. So bright, so illuminated. All you must do is tap into that through your own special process. We can serve as your witnesses, we can let you borrow some of our bravery as you make your way. The time will certainly come when we will ask to borrow some of yours, for all of us, no matter where we are on the path are bound to get discouraged and forget the things we thought we knew and so we must be reminded.

When you are born you are open, accessible. When you experience pain you become even more hollow. If you experience pain of the chronic sort that hollowness becomes transparent, you may feel as if you cease to be and so we run for external things to fill up the transparency within so that we may feel again because in feeling we know that we are human and therefore we exist. With the dull hollowness of chronic pain, the omnipresent transparency that follows and the efforts to fill the void, we might get into some habits like overeating, seeking the approval of others, sex/drugs/rock & roll whatever we need to feel sensation, to make up for our lack of feeling and oftentimes we will overdo it become swayed to the other side where we become used to feeling too much and that becomes our baseline. We may start to hold onto our pain as a means of filling up the void as well and rationalize our lack of forgiveness with lots of reasons why- righteous indignation, etc. Righteous indignation is fine but please understand that it stands in the way of discovering your true baseline. Anger, frustration, rage, anguish are not your baseline. All anger does it tell you have stuff to work on.

Allow us to give you a short cut. Hollowness is your baseline. You need to be hollow for G-D to get in. If you are complete and fulfilled by self then you have no need for G-D or Goodness to work through you.

This can be a difficult concept because you are spiritually complete so why do you need to be carved out too? The process of living flexibly creates hollowness. Not rushing to fill up on something creates space so that you are free to relate outside of learned habits and impressions.

One of the best pieces of spiritual advice we ever got was to always remain a little bit hungry. This works in marvelous ways for your waistline and sex life of course but the spiritual ramifications are what we're examining here… It is spiritual to need and desire G-D above all things.

It is spiritual to allow space to move within you for God to work magic in your life. Your wildest dreams are easily accomplished when you are moving in the right direction.

How do you get moving in the right direction?

By slowing down. By coming to a full stop, a concrete analysis of where you are, what you want and what's in between. By pausing to feel the space within you that is God and is capable of exacting the most precious of miracles right before your very eyes. Think of yourself as having your very own remote control. Visualize pressing pause and slow the eff down.

By slowing down you can meditate, you can breathe, you can see the reality of this moment. You can find great power. You can become a magnet of strength for others. Nothing is more attractive that someone who knows how to thrive despite obstacles. Someone who has tackled their own issues and endured and can therefore start to attack some of the bigger societal obstacles. Sometimes it works the other way- by attacking societal obstacles you start to conquer your own demons. Ask any present day psychologist about this.

Getting angry just bolsters your righteous indignation. It bolsters your separateness. The real strength is dealing with that conflagration of emotion that reminds you how fragile you are, how much you need God, how with God you can forgive and thrive despite all obstacles. You are so much greater than you ever imagined.

There's a saying in the recovery community- "I would've sold myself short if I maintained the list of stuff I thought I deserved when I first got sober. I had no clue how much was possible. How much stuff I didn't even realize was in front of me."

Being Orgasmic Without Assistance

Looking back, we can say, without a doubt, that there is *nothing more pathetic than a woman with the physical attributes who lacks the basic skill set.* Ladies, puh-leeze, learn how to do IT in a resilient, gutsy way. That is the fundamental difference between the women who enjoy life and those who do not.

Don't believe the lies, that sex should be shame based and unpleasant.

The two of us are living proof of what happens to women once shame's barbs no longer proved effective… Jess is with a partner who rings her bell and Reet has never settled in that area.

Remember- authentically pleasing sex increases your inspiration and creative output. Two very valuable ingredients in the pursuit of your Big Dream.

So you're not there yet… Perhaps you're a bit uncomfortable with that region "down there." Go get a vibrator, girl. Get some literature. Or perhaps get some other items from your local novelty store and don't hold back. Walk into the store like you own the place and go grab the biggest, baddest toy you can find and go up the counter with confidence and ask "what other colors does this come in?" The point here is that if you can't walk into a store and BUY a vibrator, how in the hell are you going to get the full pleasure out of using it when you get home?

Midwest women are taught to be the angel in white in and outside of the bedroom. We are "good girls". C'mon ladies, we say learn to get down and dirty with your bad self.

Sexy Mamas Of the Midwest   159
Dallas - Stapleton
Guide To Gardening Your Soul

Everything that you learn will help you relate to that one special person without abandon.

That is our goal, you see. To learn how to relate to that **one** special person with abandon.

We are not advocating that you be a slut; only a slut with yourself in the privacy of your own room. If you don't know what you want and how to get it, then how do you expect another human being to know what you want or how to give it to you?

Sex is a powerful component in a relationship. While it isn't the most important component, it certainly ranks up there! When you are with the right partner, the connection felt with your sexual chemistry can be electric and we want you to experience all that you deserve.

Learn what you like. Learn what makes you scream. Understand your body and get comfortable with it. Nobody wants to have sex with a woman who only wants to lay on her back, avoid oral and do it in the dark. Yupperino- that missionary porn industry is just booming these days, isn't it?

And Oh about the "O"….. Ladies you are only doing yourselves harm by lying about it.

You are never going to teach your dude how to give you that favorite vowel "O O O O O" if you pretend the boring little move he just pulled actually did it for you. Everyone is familiar with the scene in "When Harry Met Sally" when Sally fakes the orgasm. We are not into the fake. If you fake it, you get what you deserve.

He will also get an inflated sense of his abilities and be confused when he can't deliver to the next woman (if indeed you are not his last) when he tries this "full proof" move again.

Do yourself a favor. Tell the truth. If he asks if you had the "O" and you didn't then say "NO".

And another thing…

For all you gorgeous middle aged women out there at the top of your game who are reading this book to gain tips on keeping your man interested. Say your believe your man is drawn to a 19 year old without your worldly experience. So what. It won't last, trust us. In the immortal words of Jessica's husband, "What am I going to do with an 18 year old other than lose interest?"

Do you remember what you were like when you first entered into the sexual realm? Pretty darned self absorbed, self conscious to clearly articulate what you wanted in the sack. That pretty young thing wants to do IT with another pretty young thing like she is, if she's bothering with your dude at all it's only because she's after his acquisitions and not him and he'll catch onto sooner than later. Stand by and laugh darlings. Take him for all he's worth and get yourself a little cougar action. We guarantee that you'll
   (a) appear more attractive to your ex
   (b) be having better sex than your ex is cuz men are more virile when they're younger, women are just the opposite. You're going to get "drilled" while he lays with a dead fish
   (c) do well in the divorce settlement as you make your way toward your godly equivalent- a man who doesn't run around on his wife who is age appropriate for where you're at.

After all, the Chinese character for crisis embodies two qualities- both danger and opportunity. Make the most of your ex's low self esteem and upgrade to a better model. He sounds like a lame-o anyway.

Prescribing the Cause

How many times do we reach for the quick fix when pain comes?

Headache? Go for the Tylenol. Depression? Hide under the covers. Heartache? Go for the cheesecake.

What we would like to see happen is a subtle shift.

A pause if you will between feeling the feeling
>   (headache/depression/heartache)
and your reaction
>   (Tylenol/Bedspread/Cheesecake).

Are you a reactor?

Someone approaches you. Wants to get on your case about something or some one. They jump down your pretty little throat and guess what-you jump down theirs. Now that pretty little throat ain't so pretty. You've taken on the other party's mood = anger. You've absorbed their feelings because you don't know your own.

We see all too often the person who flits back and forth between these two states of "I'm great" to "I'm miserable".

These women are definite reactors. They allow others to determine the course of their day. Remember when we talked about lying to ourselves? These gals have not un-learned the art of lying. They have a thought which evokes a fear which immediately prescribes a new mood. These women need to avoid the negative images thrust at them from the media. They are not ready to absorb it all. As friends of these types, we can help by reminding them that the media and the

East and West coast images aren't realistic goals by any standard and help her get back to center.

When we are a perpetual mystery to ourselves we are shit at defense.

We move from fear. We overreact. We freak out on people, most specifically ourselves.
We resist uncovering the mystery of self because it takes work. Because it's not so pretty all the time. Because it is easier to be addicted to feeling poorly.

Feeling poorly keeps the vice of pain tight. We resist the urge to do the deep dive inside because we feel we lack the courage. We feel we lack the courage because we don't know our center.

Shortcut: Your center is G-D.

That center has unlimited power. That center can transform even the harshest of circumstances.

You'd never believe it but when we you stop pouring negativity down your hatch you stop feeling poorly. The majority of life should be spent in neutral. Not a place of Polly Purehearted Put On Positivity but a place of neutrality where you can focus on what you want and achieve your dreams.

Here's the thing with Polly Purehearts for the most part. They have resisted our steps much in the same way that the Negativity Addicts (aka Drama Queens) have, just in a slightly more creative way. They are the folks who have read The Secret and believe in what is has to say (which is awesome, by the way) but they have skipped over the work of releasing the past by assuming that they are moving from a place of neutrality and transformation.

And in all fairness, perhaps that is true for some. Perhaps some folks who have been raised in the wilderness, unaffected by societal norms (religion/laws/psychology) can do just that. However, the majority of us cannot. We've got a head full of shoulds and should nots that have become our cognitive map for living life and even something as powerful as the Secret cannot undo all of our yesterdays as miraculously as we would like.

Life is tough. If you're not touching in at center for rest and pause in the midst of all that living, you are not renewing yourself, you are not growing. You find the center of being so that you can find rationality, you can find peace and ease, you can figure out who you are as an individual who is striving for more than what you were born into.

So here's the thing with the other side of thinking, with Drama Queens, as we call them.

They don't know where they end and others begin. They are unintentionally toxic wastelands. The Drama Queen is much too busy stewing in present day negativity and past inadequacies to meet the healing they have at center, the chance to actually be free.

You cannot be cool with yourself, your center if you are afraid of what it looks like.

You cannot determine your true baseline (LCD) until you accept all of you, past and present. An authentic being is trapped inside.

Your past will continue to repeat itself. Your present will continue to be drama-tic because you have not harnessed the power of the still small voice inside of you. You haven't harnessed the power of discernment.

We are discerning women when we choose more of the positive to incorporate into our lives. Sure we may slip up and engage in a bitch fest or show up late to work one day in order to hide under the covers for a bit, but, for the most part, we support positive processes out of negative emotions.

Sexy Mamas Of the Midwest   164
Dallas - Stapleton
Guide To Gardening Your Soul

We give ourselves the chance to break free from old patterns and the bullshit people told us as kids.

It is just not attractive to go from in control to curled up on the garage floor bawling your eyes out because your husband bought the wrong brand of laundry soap or your friend didn't comment on your facebook page. Life is not conspiring against you. Your husband didn't buy the wrong soap on purpose. Your friends are not talking behind your back and the family is not "against" you. Your emotional self is just wringing its hands with sinister delight that it has battled your soul and won!

Short cut: You are not a kid now, honey. The tears that you cry should be "big girl tears," not the tears or rants of the broken teenager inside you. You are able to claim your grown up sensibilities. You are able to take more responsibility for your own life. You can pull that miserable little girl out of her unfortunate circumstances by choosing not to keep repeating past mistakes. Let her know she is safe in your care. You are in charge and things are unfolding as they should.

Why do we do a SWOT analysis? So we can see our patterns from the past dictating our present. Why do we do our LCD status? So we can see the direction and flow of our energy. We can see where we're wasting potential healing.

Your present reality is the degree to which you have effectively dealt with your baggage. It is perfectly realistic to have everything you've ever dreamed of if you are ready to harness the unlimited bravery inside of your and deal with your *stuff*. If you deny your stuff is there or have suppressed a lot of it, your body and mind are blocking the flow of your spirit. The spirit cannot emerge in a blocked system.

When you have a symptom (headache/depression/heartache) begin to prescribe the cause (underlying issue) rather than the symptom.

Instead of reaching for the cheesecake, ask yourself, what is this feeling of emptiness trying to teach me?

Your symptoms are clues, not barriers to change. Your symptoms are short cuts to greater realization of your dreams. Sitting on the mountaintop squishing all of your symptoms will get you nowhere in the long run. It is good to be flawed and to exhibit those flaws clearly because then you know what to work on.

When a symptom (pain) arises, it suggests ever so subtly or no- that the best thing to do is to slow down and move closer toward acceptance. Acceptance doesn't mean that you like the symptom. Acceptance is merely acknowledging the symptom as your present day reality. When you slow down long enough to accept what is hurting you, you are able to try to learn from it (uncover your patterns) and ask for help if that pain becomes too overwhelming.

You don't need to hire a personal trainer to look fabulous.

You don't need to go to India for a spiritual experience.

You have all of the knowledge you will ever need blanketed within you in a special code that only time and bravery will translate. Time comes with age. Bravery with God.

Influence vs. Dominance

Those at peace with their own reality don't find it necessary to exert control over others. This is true in our romantic relationships with men. If you are a strong, confident, sexy woman who has found her inner joy and your know how to love yourself, you will not find joy in forcing your partner into submission. You'll instead, enjoy a balance in your relationship.

Men may behave like children or dogs at times; however, that doesn't give us the inalienable right to treat them as such. We are hear to tell you, if you treat a man like a child or bark at him like a dog, he will continue to act like one and he will rebel against you. This is not a partnership that will sustain.

There is a difference between influence and dominance and you, ladies, need to learn and become skilled at the difference. Influence is sexy, dah-leengs.

People who are skilled at influence avoid "telling". Your tone and your spirit can motivate any man to move mountains and make you appear sexy in his eyes. Or, at least he'll empty the dishwasher or pick up the dry cleaning on the way home.

In order to influence a man, we just need to learn to approach him in a way that he will "think" it was his idea, by allowing him a choice in the matter, or do so in a way that he perceives that he is being the "man" by helping us out.

Remember: Men are hunters NOT gatherers. They want to provide. They do not want to be stripped of their masculinity in their cave. How do we get a man to "provide" when it is our idea?

Imagine this: You want your husband to pick up the dry cleaning on the way home from work. In your quest to get through your busy day, your typical approach might be to just get this task off your check list by calling him up and authoritatively saying "I need you to pick up the dry-cleaning".

Do you know what he hears??

Him: Mom just gave me a chore! Uga-waaaaaaaaaaaaaaaaaaaaa!

What if you tried in a nurturing voice: "Hi honey, is it possible that you could pick up the dry-cleaning for me on the way home? It would really help me out"

Do you know what he hears??

Him: My sweet lady needs my help, it's time to get my superhero cape and save the day!

C'mon ladies, we are intelligent and influence others at work, why not our husbands/partners?

What if I need a picture hung on the wall?

"Hang that picture over the fireplace and don't forget to use the molly bolt".

The message? Not only do I want you to do it, but you are such an idiot that I need to tell you HOW to do it.

How about trying something different like, "[Sigh]... I tried to hang this picture up, but I didn't know where you kept your hammer and then I wasn't sure if I needed a molly bolt". Whoo Hoo.... Big strong man needs to get out his TOOLS for me!

Sexy Mamas Of the Midwest   168
Dallas - Stapleton
Guide To Gardening Your Soul

Now, we know most of you grew up knowing how to change a tire, operate power tools and can hang a picture. The point is, you need to allow a man to participate in a relationship instead of being a martyr and doing it all yourself. Otherwise, you are just creating a situation where you are not sexy.

The reason a man is so dreamy and attentive when you first meet is he is still thinking of you as that untapped piece of Sexy Mama that he can't wait to explore and tear into bite after bite each night. As soon as you take on the role of "mother" you will leave the role of "sexy mama" behind. How can a man look forward to coming home to his "mother" each night? What could be more emasculating than to be sitting at work where you are considered a top dog, only to be phoned by your wife/girlfriend and be torn a new ass because you forgot to take out the trash?
Ladies, you don't win over a man by shaming him, belittling him and ordering him to serve.

It is so simple and yet we so easily fall into this trap and it is difficult to get out of it. In our quest to have everything run smoothly in a relationship or a household, we take on all of the roles and try to wear all of the hats. We are not saying that he isn't a shit face for leaving the chores or duties or child rearing up to you, but if you are completely honest with yourself, didn't you allow it to morph into that?? Was it that way right from the beginning? Did you set the expectation right from the get-go? Or, did you set the expectations so effing high that he failed right out of the starting blocks? You need to figure out a way to get what you want out of him and have him see you as that sexy mama he married or chose to date!

Yes, he may be giving you lots of reasons to treat him like a little boy, but please don't fall into the trap… please! Don't equate your husband/partner with one of the children. Once you do, he is now looking at you as his mother and he isn't going to come home and have mad, passionate, monkey sex with his mama.

We all love the alpha male. He is strong, confident, and steps up in the relationship. Yes, we love this…. Until he doesn't take our crap anymore. Men don't like pushy women. They don't find it sexy.

Short Cut: Treat him like a man so he will in turn treat you like the sexy woman that you are.

Why do some men have affairs? To prove their manliness. Think about it. The mistress doesn't treat him like a child. She doesn't order him around and complain, bitch, moan, etc. about him. She gets to show him her sexy side and he then gets to feel like a man again. Why let the under-developed among us have our partners?

Why do some women have affairs? Because at work, they are appreciated. The men don't see their "home life persona". They see this strong sexy confident woman and they flirt with her and give her attention. She is not barking at them to pick up their dirty socks because they do what they are supposed to do! The attention she gets from them is not being received at home and suddenly she is getting fulfilled elsewhere. She is treated like a woman.

Stop this cycle! Get into your roles and embrace them. There is nothing wrong with allowing a man to be a man and giving him the opportunity to lead a home. There is nothing wrong with you being a sexy woman who is a partner to her sexy husband/partner.

We are not saying that by giving him the opportunity to lead that he is "better". He is just "different" and by respecting that, you are actually appearing sexier to him than you can imagine! Please don't compete with each other. It is not healthy. Partners don't compete, they build each other up and they want more for the other person then they want for themselves.

Why is it that you want him to step up in an emergency and take control and be the "man", but in daily aspects of the relationship, you want to control things?? Why is it that in THOSE moments, it is OK for him to be the man? How confusing for men that we shift the roles over and over. We want to be their "equals" and then we get pissed if they don't open the door for us. Let's face it, they aren't always very clued in and we are constantly throwing curve balls and changing the rules of the game. What if suddenly the rule became that you had to do a cartwheel as you crossed home plate and nobody told you this rule until after you thought you scored a homerun?

Example: We can't stop thinking about the well known reality show couple with the gazillion kids. They were a disaster waiting to happen. He let her dominate because he was too lazy to fulfill his role. It is our contention that Jon has rebelled against this controlling, dominating spouse. He even stated that he let Kate rule the roost for too long and that he is now standing up for himself. There are rumors of an affair in the midst of a messy divorce. Look ladies, we are not condoning this man's immature behavior and his willingness to abandon his marriage and put his 8 children through a divorce. We are also not bashing Kate for being so dominating. We believe that Jon is that rare breed of man that CHOOSES a dominating spouse, who allows it because he isn't ready to grow up and truly wants a mama, who wants his spouse to control everything and make all decisions.   The problem here is this: Kate loved the role of dominating. Had she been an intelligent, sexy, self assured woman, she would have seen this train wreck coming and said "oh no, John, I am not going to do everything and control everything just so you can put your head in the sand for the next X years".   What are we saying? He wanted to be dominated and she wanted to dominate. He got sick of being dominated when he finally hit the age of 32 and now he is stuck with a woman who he no longer can find sexy because she has been his mother for 10 years.   She liked dominating. She didn't trust him to make decisions (even to going shopping because he forgot to use a coupon); she didn't let him pick out clothes for the kids, etc. She treated him like an idiot and she enabled him to take on the role of child and dog. They are both at fault and we BEG of you not to allow this to happen to you. Now he has a 22 year old girlfriend and Kate has her "show." We ask you, where did the LOVE go?

Shortcut: The minute you start acting like his mother or his older sister your man will shut the eff down, possibly to never return again. Be forewarned.

If your spouse/partner seems to be complacent with you "doing everything", don't use this as your excuse to be the controlling one. It will one day backfire. It is the Kate8 syndrome! Instead, recognize this in him and teach him to fish!

What was Kate avoiding by doing these compulsive activities? What was she forgetting about her fulfillment in trying to control everything that her child put into her mouth? We would argue that she was actually quite lazy. By compulsively engaging in minute to minute business you get to forgo what you are about? Martyrs are actually a bit lazy. Are you forgetting about yourself and your needs? Wouldn't you rather be making pottery or on a beach somewhere?

Shortcut: Do what makes you happy first and everything else, including your relationship will fall into place.

Remember, you will never win over a man by shaming, belittling or demeaning him. Is that how he would win you over?

The Elevator Speech

If you are an adult woman and are reading this book, we are going to assume you have been on at least 1 or more dates for reference. You're sitting at the dinner table and you are longing to connect with this virtual stranger and a natural means for a woman to connect is verbally. The man is physical. Now, he knows he has to play the game and ask the obligatory first date questions. If you can keep this rule in mind when you answer those questions you will already be on the path success.

Men will converse about facts. Women will reveal facts and then delve into their feelings about those facts. A sexy, wickedly intelligent women knows how to approach a dating situation without baring her emotional soul and sending out the "high maintenance" signal or the "oh shit" factor.

A man isn't interested in your long winded answers and he will more likely zone out. He is there to simply determine whether you have a good sense of humor, requisite intelligence, aren't a psychopath, are low maintenance and are showing signs of physical attraction

Take if from us, a man loves it if you keep the focus on HIM. This doesn't mean that you need to talk only about him. It means, don't flirt with the waiter. Pay attention to your date. Look him in the eye, flirt with him, and be playful. You need to have conversation, not recite your resume or gab on nonsensically.

If he compliments you, a confident, self assured woman will accept it with grace. It will turn him off if you shrug it off or tell him why his compliment doesn't apply to you. Of course you have pretty eyes!

Yes, you look amazing. Believe it. Own it. Your own perception of yourself is the first thing that others see.

So what is the biggest culprit in a dating situation that inspires women to turn a dinner table into a therapist's couch? LACK OF PREPARATION!

Let us ask you this: You just got a call for your dream job. It is everything you have ever wanted. The right salary, benefits, hours and you would absolutely fall head over heels for this job. Would you show up without prepared answers to the interview questions? We hope you are not that stupid! If you are, you don't deserve the job and we question why they called you in the first place! You certainly would not show up wearing something uncomfortable or inappropriate, and we hope you wouldn't tell a prospective employer that you were abused a child or that your husband ran away with his secretary and left you with 3 children and you really need this job to support them.

You need to prepare for your first date in the same way. A prepared woman is a classy woman. She knows what to expect and she is confident. Her natural spontaneity emerges from her sense of preparedness and is communicated through her nonverbal interactions.

If the date is going well, the body language and the experience will take precedence over the quality or lack of verbal interactions. How many times have you heard someone come off of a great date and say "it was so wonderful it was like we knew each other forever and we talked about nothing"? It just comes naturally when people connect through other means.

Do you want to know how to sustain silence? Do our steps again…

The silence must be viewed as an opportunity to let the non-verbal communication come to the forefront. What do we mean by this? FLIRT YOUR ASS OFF! A word about flirting: There is flirting and there is slutty. A flirting gesture is girlish, demure, sweet, playful and somewhat naïve. You can flirt with a man in front of his mother. A slutty gesture is raunchy, desperate, lacks class and tells everyone in the room including your date "go ahead, touch and take". Now, if that is what you want to portray, please stop reading this book immediately as we can not help you. We are professional classy women who are eager to perpetuate more professional classy women. Sluts need not apply or transformation needed.

We realize that not all of you are comfortable with the standard Q&A portion of the first date and you may often fall prey to your natural instinct to reveal your entire life history to your date. Let us impart our wisdom and experience on you so that you can prepare yourself and walk into these situations with confidence.

We use a term in business called an "Elevator Speech". It is a prepared statement or presentation that will grab someone's attention in the 30 seconds it takes to ride in an elevator. There are topics that are going to come up on a first date and we want you to prepare your Elevator Speeches so you can present your self in a way that makes him want to know more about you! These statements do not dwell on the past! An Elevator Speech is forward thinking and so should you be as a sexy, wickedly intelligent woman. You will ooze confidence if you follow these guidelines.

We have compiled a list of topics that we believe will provide you the optimum opportunity to flirt, connect and, demonstrate your enough about yourself to leave him wanting more! While this is not an all-encompassing list, it is a good guide for becoming prepared with Elevator Speeches.

- Where you're from.

- Basic Family make-up (#of siblings, if you are oldest/youngest, etc)

- University and educational experiences, omit the partying, please.

- Sports – don't try to fake it and don't overdo it. If you don't know a lot about sports like Jessica, ask him what he likes and offer to learn, even if, like Jessica you don't retain any of it because you find it mind-numbing.

- If politics are brought up – say you float towards the center.

- Traveling you've done, omit who with.

- Movies/Plays you've recently seen. Omit the chick flicks and cartoons please.

- Music you enjoy. Omit the death metal and gangsta rap.

To help you prepare, we've provided a sample conversation below. Typical first date stuff between you and a dude. Can you tell us when your character goes off course?

Him: Tell me about your family...

You: I have the typical middle-class family. My dad's great. My mom is an inspiration. I'm the oldest of 3 children. How about you?

Him: My brother and sister live in Phoenix with my mom. My dad's here in Columbus-

You: Really? My parents divorced too. I was 12. It was really hard on me because I was so close to my dad and he just took off for a long time. It really affected me. I'm pretty close to my brother, but my sister lives out of town and she never comes to visit. We really competed with each other growing up. I wish she'd come to town more because I miss my nieces and nephews. I love kids and want a ton of them.

Stop!!!!!! This is wrong on so many levels! First of all, you just jumped in and assumed his parents are split, only to go to dumping your bizarre baggage on a dude who doesn't know you. This is not a confident, sexy woman and her date will not be interested in learning more about her because he will already have learned all he needs to know. His male instinct is kicking in and it is telling him to "run." Want more on no-no conversations? Surely! We've provided a list of no-no's for you to observe in the preliminary stages of dating.

By the way, we swear on everything holy that we will appear magically at your first date and rip your vocal cords out and shove them in your water glass if you say or refer to any of the following:

- Your ex husband's bad habits
- Your unrealized ambitions
- Your gastric bypass surgery
- Your plastic surgery or augmentations or desire to have them
- The pony you never got as a child
- Your father's new mistress or 20-something-year-old wife
- Your childhood abuse
- Your dead-end job
- The boss you hate
- Your freaky dietary habits
- Your penchant for some sort of sexual position – in fact, sex at all
- An addiction or "ism"… alcohol, drug, sex, porn
- Your many divergent personalities
- Sibling rivalry
- Holiday nightmares with family
- Things that paint you as a greedy bitch (material possessions)
- You salary

- You last relationship and all its failures
- Your last relationship and on and on .anything beyond "great guy didn't work out
- Your emotional problems
- How many exes you have
- Religion
- Politics
- Family dysfunction
- Death – my grandpa just died.
- Passionate feelings about issues – we don't care if you want to save trees
- Don't announce you're a vegetarian – just don't order meat. Let him bring it up.
- Do not use the word "relationship"
- Don't complain

Homework: We recommend that you complete our 10 Steps to Gardening the Soul before embarking on any new dating situations. You will be presenting the authentic you and will be leaving the baggage out of the equation. What a wonderful opportunity for you to unleash your Sexy Mama! Men Beware!

Vulnerability

Males love to save, but they don't want to save from the "get go".

Men also love a woman with a few screws loose.

It's a difficult quality to pinpoint, that elusiveness that renders a woman irresistible. Why are we still drawn to women like Marilyn Monroe, etc…?

It's their vulnerability.

That being said, let's choose to learn from Marilyn rather than emulate her.

Vulnerability comes from authenticity. Living authentically means that you are living as closely as possible to the realization of you that your higher power intends.

When we choose to be vulnerable we're not shouting out to the world "save us." We're confirming to ourselves, to our Higher Power and to a trusted few that we are in fact human, that we are affected by life's events, but that we are currently striving to remain hopeful. We're living in constant contact with a power greater than ourselves that sustains us through all times, good and bad.

We all have our hard luck stories. We've all been through the ringer. We can let these experiences remind us of our inherent vulnerability as human beings but they don't need to rob us of our God-given bravery.

Example: Jessica, your co-author/therapist, met a client recently who sat across from her spouting off all the reasons why she was a bad ass and her *reasoning was pretty darned justified*. This girl had literally been through hell. Intergenerational poverty, abuse of all shapes and sizes, nonconsensual sex from an extremely early age, racism, drug addiction, had her children taken away from her by the state – enough pain to inspire a narcissist. Big surprise- she was one. Here's the thing with most narcissists though, Sexy Mamas don't buy their tale for a second. So Jessica didn't believe this girl's structure of self sufficiency either. Narcissists are funny creatures in that they move about the world as if they are in an orb- failing to interact with the circumstances around them, the present experience, because they are so wrapped up in the story line of appearing to have it all together or conversely to be a freak of nature… And in the midst of all of the acting, they know fundamentally that they are frauds but it makes them work even harder to keep the façade up. Jessica knew this girl's m.o. very well, because she had personal experience with all this. She looked across the table at the girl spinning her web of how effed up she was and said to her, "Perhaps you're not as bad as you've been led to believe. Perhaps your personal myth doesn't at all resemble what's really going on inside. Perhaps you should stop believing that you're too poor, too black, too drug addicted, too devastated by abuse because it doesn't serve you. It is your choice, you know."

After all, how does one even begin to get to the good stuff in life when you are distracted by all of your surface bru-ha-ha?

This chick was so invested in appearing antisocial that she had forgotten the truth of the matter. She had forgotten that she still had a soul, a conscience, and that she had been lying to herself by perpetuating a storyline that did not serve her true nature… That she was a human being who had done the best with what she was given.

No more, no less.

And for anyone to sit across the table from her and look into her eyes and witness what she was struggling against--- herself--- allowed this girl to start to reflect internally- something she hadn't done for a long while.

This girl permitted herself to look at the big picture. The real stuff. The ups and downs. The attempts and failures.

She saw her shadow and it wasn't bad. It was good.

And she started to cry.

Because she was realizing in the midst of all of this struggling that she was enough. That she had always been enough. That it- living- perpetuating in the struggle with an open heart- was enough.
That she didn't need to add to her true self or diminish her true nature. That out of the box, she was just fine as is.

The girl started to cry at the suggestion that she might be freed from the story line of fucked-up-ed-ness that she'd believed her whole life. The girl cried at the thought of putting it all behind her.

That's the thing with freedom, ladies. It's right there alongside the willingness to live vulnerably in this moment. You can put aside your personal myth. You can put aside all the crap others have spun for you, even badass myth that you yourself have erected in order to sustain divisions between you and your fellow man.

Freedom is IN THIS MOMENT of reconciliation with self. Acceptance of one's humanity is one of the most powerful assertions you can make... Yes I have been through this stuff but I am choosing to exist in this moment imperfectly. I am an amalgamation of life experiences, yes, but I can choose new patterns, I can choose to remain open, I can turn to my pain, process it with trusted others and then throw it away. I do not have to believe the *stuff* people throw at me.

It is exhausting to hold onto something that you are not. To go day in and day out without your authentic self is like living without requisite air. You are barely breathing. When you can finally face you in the mirror and realize that you have survived and you like who you are and you don't have to be anything but what YOU want to be, it is freeing. No one has stolen you. You are not broken, despite all the *stuff* folks have told you.

Make up your own creation myth that authentically reflects all of you good and bad and effing believe it.

You are one of your G-D's chosen ones. You are one of G-D's beloveds. No more, no less.

Only you can do the big stuff, the deep stuff to call your soul back. Only you can save yourself. And the big save is what makes life worth living.

Affirmation: G-D loves me even when I don't love myself. I can choose to start loving myself today. I can choose to allow life to affect me for the better. I can survive my own pain. I forgive myself for not allowing the BIG LOVE in.

The Psychic Makeover

You need to be with someone who is of equal intelligence. When you are at the same intellectual level you have an even playing field.

Trust us on that one.

You need to be with someone who has similar interests.

You need to be with someone who is sane.

There seems an inherent flexibility in women. We're used to changes in our moods and feelings due to hormones. Our uterus falls out once a month. Women are used to being groundless. We're undervalued in our culture. If you harness some goal orientation, male logic with female persona you are unstoppable. When you let your female emotions take over your logic you become weak, you need to be careful who's around when you're like in that state. There are certain men who love to see a woman victimized. These are the parasites of plant life. Be forewarned.

And yet, a lot of women stick around in the dis-ease and environment of deprivation.

Example: In China there's a bizarre custom where unmarried dead women are married to living men. The body isn't exhumed or anything so don't get too disgusted but the principal is that an unmarried woman brings shame to her family if she passes into the afterlife without a male hereditary line to attach herself to.

How backward, you may be thinking, but we would argue to the contrary. So many social and cultural concepts are, in fact, very present manifestations of deep psychological truths.

We would argue that a great many western women do the psychological equivalent of a Chinese ghost marriage.

Are you staying in a bad relationship in order to avoid bringing shame to your family?

Are you imbuing your partner with qualities he doesn't possess in order to justify staying with him?

How many women do this:

> **Woman:** I want this.
>
> **Man:** That's bullshit.
>
> **Woman:** Okay... *(crestfallen)*

You need to say:

> **Woman:** Do you want this?
>
> **Man:** No.
>
> **Woman:** G-D bless you. Buh-bye. *(walks out)*

Ladies, we've all done it, including both of us. We have both stayed in relationships for far too long in order to fulfill some sort unmet need that had nothing to do with happiness or health.

Jessica stayed with an abuser because the sex was good and he had a lot of cash.

Rita stayed in a marriage for the sake of her child where her needs were not being met and things were never working.

Get off the merry go round of I can't and learn that you can.

You have a gut for a reason and if it is telling you to get out, then get out. We have instincts for a reason. If enough red flags are going up that you'd wreck havoc on the Indy 500, notice them and get the eff out.

If your friends and family are telling you to get out, listen to them. G-D speaks to us through others ALL THE TIME.
It is really easy to ignore all of the warning signs because we want to believe the good in a person, or we want to preserve our investment. Whatever the reason, a bad relationship is toxic on your health and you will start to notice physical signs, emotional symptoms and at some point you are unable to focus on the mundane normalcy in life of finances, job, family, friends because you are consumed with everyday occurrences of this toxicity.

The following statements are absolutely unacceptable for Sexy Mamas to make:

- "Yeah he has a prison record but that was ten years ago."

- "Yeah he was an IV drug user but I would never ask him to take a HIV test because I trust him."

- "Sure he has a degree and no work history but nobody's hiring and I really feel in my heart that his time is best spent working on that novel."

- "Yeah he lost his job because he tried to hit someone over the head with a fire extinguisher but it wasn't his fault. "

- "My parents hate him but they just don't know him."

- "My kids can't stand him but they just don't know that side of him."

- "That girl you saw him with was just a friend. Sure she's an exotic dancer but she's pursuing medical school and was just asking for some admissions advice."

In a healthy relationship your partner will not curse your name, quit his job in order for you to support him, or keep on drinking regardless of the consequences.

In a healthy relationship there is no debasement. There is no talking down to someone. It is an exchange between two consenting adults. Your partner will see the good in you rather than the bad. He will not perseverate on the negative qualities that you might possess. He allows you to express yourself. He allows you to be who you are. They are not threatened by your growth.

A word on verbal abuse:

We are seeing on TV a move in our culture away from respectful, loving dialogue into verbally abusive, back-biting, name calling aggressive behavior as the norm.

Not acceptable for Sexy Mamas.

Now, your authors will not say we are perfect and we haven't slung a few proverbial "F" bombs or two; however, we are appealing to all Sexy Mamas to say that name calling is NOT an expression of feelings and any man who wishes to engage in this sort of behavior should hid the road and learn some effing manners. Kablam!

A relationship should be an equal partnership and we fail to see how this is possible if one person is continually entering into a power struggle with you.

When someone uses "potty words" he is saying you don't matter, you are less than me, I play dirty and I need power.

Power struggles don't form bonds, they break them and power struggles don't nurture Sexy Mamas.

A wise priest once said to Rita:

"Your spouse's number one job is to make sure you go to heaven."

In the Christian tradition, women are viewed as God's daughters and are advised to be accorded with that level of respect by their partners.

Require that. You are your G-D's daughter.
Women love to project. We love to give makeovers- psychic and otherwise. This is a wonderful, hopeful characteristic but one you must be extremely wary of.

Don't waste your love on a relationship that's a pile of excrement. If you put in on a plate with a pretty garnish and a table cloth it's still a pile of dog shit. You can't hide a pile of dog shit. It smells like shit. Shine it up, it's still a turd.

But what about the metaphysical component in all this, you may ask?

Yes, it is important to add increasing amounts of love to your relationship through the act of loving that person, faults and all but don't be a moron. This principal applies to folks who have perhaps "fallen out of love" a bit, not to wife beaters who get their self esteem from abusing their partners.

You need a professional's help.

Part Four: Meditations

Recommitting & Focusing Daily

In order to accomplish a dream you must focus.

It takes a tremendous amount of energy to make things happen. We hope by now, you believe you deserve good things.

And in the flurry of accomplishing your dreams, your move toward focused energy, lots of tumult may spring up as the shift in your energy, the focus required to maintain that shift requires an offset of opposite level energy.

In short, if you are doing what you should be doing, lots of gross shit will fly your way.

It's a means of reminding you that you are on the right path.

Sure you may think, wow how is this happening just when I'm doing such great stuff? Why is the negative hunting me down like a magnet?

Because negative charges are attracted to positive energy. That's the importance of not overindulging in false positivity- you will become a magnet for sociopaths. Trust us, we've attracted our share.

Finding your roots, your neutrality is where the power is, where the compassion lives. Being able to look at things on both sides of the spectrum equally and relate but not have it alter your fundamental groundedness.

You get your wisdom from neutrality. Not picking sides, not being thrust into certain mind sets out of obligation or wanting to belong. Sexy Mamas are too intelligent to pick sides. We form our own opinions on our own time based on our values, spirit and beliefs.

You get your spirituality from neutrality. It's not good or bad that your dude checks out some sweet young thing. It just is. Your reaction is a clue to the deeper issues you harbor inside.

Lots of times we project our feelings onto other people. The whole story of the medical student believing she has symptoms of the illness she's studying? Whatever is in the forefront of our mind we have the tendency to project.

So make it a point to have groundedness in the forefront of your mind. It will sustain you. You will identify with people, you will have reservoirs of compassion to give, and you will be able to change amazingly because you have boundless energy when you are feeding off your source.

When you are feeding off fake positivity you are faking yourself out. You can't effort your way into a spiritual experience. Fake positivity requires so much work. Honesty, dealing with what's really there and undying connection to your G-D is what transforms not a bullshit Pollyanna approach to living that you don't really believe in anyway.

We are advocating a depth experience of living. One that denies the surface oriented side of things. Resist the urge to paint pretty pictures of living in order to keep up the pretense of perfection. Perfection hurts. Perfection denies your spirit its full expression. Perfection inhibits freedom. Perfection is not fearless.

Life is not perfect. Life is a growth experience. When you pretend otherwise you are denying your humanity. You are cloaking yourself in an impenetrable force field. You are being pathological. The greatest healers are the ones who are still wounded themselves but working with honesty in their hearts, cognizant of their shortcomings.

Anger

Anger can be your best bud. It can keep you alive and kicking. It can motivate you. It can become a close companion.

Anger can give you a will to live when everyone else has turned their backs on you.

Anger can be a flame of survival. Anger is a good thing if used properly.

It is good to be principled. To see things that offend you and say so. It is never excusable for a child to be abused, for a woman or man to be raped, for old folks to live in poverty. We see all too much of this in the media.

Anger is a tremendously energetic element that can get your engines going.

The key is what you do with that energy.

Are you using that energy to bring about centered change or are you using that energy to bring your ego into greater focus and admiration?

It can wake you up. You can use your anger as a means of unlocking the secrets of your heart rather than as an obstacle preventing you from ascending the mountaintop.

When you feel the familiar surge, talk to it. What is your anger trying to tell you? What are you fighting against?

Is it truly someone else? Or is it just an aspect of yourself, an aspect of some unresolved issue that you haven't made peace with?

Anger is inspiring. It can convince us of our own strength, our ability to endure unbelievable offenses.
But in most instances, we use our anger as a means of getting a cheap high on our own steam. We used it as a means of polarizing us from others, of keeping our individuality intact.

Let us tell you something.

There is no health in separation. There is no benefit to being a bitch, in the long-run. You just come across as frigid and scary.

The trouble is our society tells us, as women, that anger is something to be feared and so we tend to overreact when we encounter it as a defense mechanism, a means of keeping ourselves safe.

We're told that anger isn't Godly, that it isn't maternal or sisterly, that we should forgive and forget and so we force that upon ourselves, that forced forgiveness of others and end up angry with us rather than them.

Eff that, we say.

Let the anger fall where it is supposed to. Let it fall quickly and with justice and then let it go. Express it appropriately. Express it in a healthy manner, in a way that does not damage you or others.

We are entitled as human beings to the full on expression of complicated emotions.

We are not living in the middle ages all hushed and quiet. We are not living in Victorian times blanketed in neuroses and sex obsessed. We are not living in the 70's full of pomp and circumstance and rigid beliefs in what needs to happen.

We have no effing idea what's going to happen. We are human beings living in God's world. The world is an extension of God and the world as God is doing just fine.

Don't take your cues from the world and its injustices. Take your cues from God.

Jesus smashed the idols to the floor in a fit of fury. He really did. We're not kidding. Jesus was a great dude but Jesus was no effing doormat.

These were great men. It's time to make some great women. We're long overdue.

By the way, we are not giving you a free pass to act like a raving lunatic. Please don't go around busting up chairs and smashing your boyfriend's car windows only to say that the Sexy Mamas told you to. There is anger and there is rage. We are not advocating a psycho drama rage fest. Get real with your bad self and use the energy of your anger for direction. Channel it into passion, into source energy to accomplish your Big Dream, your life's mission.

Don't use it as an excuse to hide from your pain. Use it as a means of increasing awareness and compassion with your fellow beings.

Neutrality

Cultivating neutrality is a means of establishing distance between what you have and what you want. It's a means of examining the past, present, anticipating the future.

It's a means of acceptance, not necessarily approval.

We need to, at some point accept that our father molested us as a kid, if he did. We don't have to approve of it or think that it's okay for it to have happened but if we are to get better we need to accept it.

We will often times go through the process of healing and in healing we will confront the stages of grief, those things that Elizabeth Kubler Ross identified:

Anger
Denial
Depression
Acceptance
The last one but we can't remember it right now

The point?... When we get to the end of the healing cycle of grief we arrive at neutrality. We arrive at a place of truth.

We're not clinging to our old pain as a means of filling up the void within. We know where the void goes, what the void means, the void goes straight to the divine.

We don't need to fill the void within us with fat, lazy, lying activities.

We don't need to fill the void within us with meaningless endeavor, with things that don't fit us. We fill the void within us with our shortcuts to knowing who we are like:

Creativity
Meditation
Service
Conservation of Energy

In inviting an attitude of neutrality into your life you're not saying no to positivity. You're not saying no to negativity. You're accepting the world, with all of its quirks as is.

Neutrality is a practical means of living in this world. Neutrality inspires an attitude of inquisitiveness, problem solving, and courage to go deep and know who we are and where others begin.

Neutrality is not the same as apathy. It is not refusing to take part in the activity of compassion for others; it is not avoiding real world responsibility. Neutrality allows you to become effective because you are not taking on someone else's shit, you are taking up the mantle of self, the highest calling any being can possibly attain.

The mantle of self is 100% unique. It is charged, it is found through trials and tribulations, through successes and glories. It is found through accomplishing great things with the energy of G-D working through you in this, a very human world.

Neutrality allows you to keep a clear head while you're working for the healing of others. It helps you become involved in processes that are genuine to your being. Each of us has a special calling. Neutrality allows you to slow down long enough to rid yourself of the opinions and "shoulds" of others to allow the still small voice to inspire you and drive you further into the next phase of development.

Neutrality is not sitting in judgment of anyone or anything for too long. It is good to know right from wrong for you in terms of personal code and effectiveness, but it is not your place to preach anything to others other than inspiration and courage.

Inspiration and courage can reach others when we speak of our own process of decoding our past, of unlearning our pain. Inspiration is doing something we never thought ourselves capable of doing. Inspiration is, in short, *the applauded path of self realization.* Being inspired regularly releases you from the boredom of not realizing your dreams. You are inspiring to others when you begin to realize and manifest your dreams, your highest calling. Being inspiring to others releases them from the boredom of not realizing their dreams and encourages them to pick up where they left off. Inspiration, simply speaking is refusing to engage in fat, lazy, lying activities.

You know the truth of what's going on with you, fundamentally, underneath all the bru ha ha anyone's ever told you. You know what you want, what you need, what you currently have and what's in between.

Your conscience, which we would argue is actually your higher self speaking to you, is a means of revealing what your truth actually is.

When you work against your conscience, you will keep track of it, you will remember, you will punish yourself or reward yourself accordingly.

You are creating your own reality with the degree to which you are aligning yourself with your conscience, with your still small voice.

You may go through your whole life unaware of what the still small voice actually wants and needs.

Cut that *stuff* out.

Gain access to the still small voice by shutting down all the chaos of the ups and downs the ins and outs the rationalization, the stuck up in your head-ness. Slow the eff down; find your power in neutrality, your roots, your own unique systems and opinions.

Find health in distancing yourself from everything you think you believe. It is your right to choose what you want to be. You can unlearn anything. You can gain any skill. But you can't lie to yourself. It's a complete waste of god-given energy.

Neutrality isn't some mountaintop you ascend as a result of present day work you do. Neutrality is a present day decision to distance yourself through service, meditation, conservation of energy from past events.

Neutrality is a means of moving forward today.

Homework: Draw a bridge from where you started when you began this book to where you'd like to be someday. Draw yourself on that bridge. What is standing in your way? How far do you have to go? When you see folks who have made major life changes it is a result of thinking the same way daily. Great things are achieved on a daily basis. Slow down in order to keep moving.

Feed your soul, your distance from emotionality in order to keep participating.

Think of your landscape daily, your landscape being the tone of your inner voice. Try to keep this voice consistent with where you want to take your Soul. Listen to your landscape and adjust what you are doing if your voice becomes off.

Distance is the suggestion that you are not your emotions. You are not wrapped up in a big bru ha ha 24/7. It is the suggestion that you are more than the ups and downs, that there is a constant in there somewhere, that there is a baseline that can offer far more comfort than the heaping of things you think are you in an effort to protect yourself from the assault of others.

You are so much more capable of dealing with the world when you are grounded and proactive. When you don't sink into sympathy but empathy because you know where you begin and others end.

About Us

We've chosen to add this section at the end to give you an idea where we've come from in our individual journeys thus far.

It might also give you, as our readers, an opportunity to see how uniquely suited to this profession we are… After all, we are Becoming as well…

Jessica…

Hello there, loves. Reflecting over the course of my life is always a bit hilarious as it was a sort of fast-forward, high speed dubbing existence (you know that button on the old tape players that you could press and make your favorite Paula Abdul album sound like a bunch of chipmunks singing?)—well that was my life for a long time. Ultimately it didn't work out too well but we'll get to that eventually…

I've had a few incarnations in this life. I started out a very fearful, nerdy, skinny little thing who would gaze at photos of women like Marilyn Monroe and get lost in a daydream. Every night after everyone was asleep I would pray for two things:

(1) Deliver me G-D from my genetic history
and
(2) Please G-D give me boobs like all the bombshell archetypes and while you're at it, saw off my pale, long legs and make me spritely and gymnastic-looking like all the girls at school who call me names.

Neither prayer was answered and I thank my G-D for it today. You see, loves, my biggest problem was evaluating myself from the male perspective rather than my own and wouldn't you know it I was delivered from that mentality after a *roller coaster ride of sex, drugs and performance art...* (I wish I could say rock & roll but I'm not musically talented in the slightest)... Instead, I was a little alternative art chick who had trouble paying her rent and did lots of drugs to cope with the inevitable schism that occurs when one is engaging in activities outside of their moral code to **pay** said rent. I cracked up pretty badly at age 23 and locked myself in my apartment for about 3 weeks, ordering nothing but Chinese food and entertaining a delusion that the FBI was spying on me through the sprinkler system in the ceiling. After I cracked up definitively, the passion for Chinese food dissipated as did my FBI perseveration and *for the first time in my life I understood that I wasn't completely nuts.* It was **le premier fois** when I didn't taste fear in the back of my throat. The worst thing that could ever happen- cracking up- had taken place and I had survived. I had nothing left to fear from anyone or anything. For the first time in my life I could choose who I wanted to be. Yes, I could see the spiritual benefits to being a "hot mess" for some time because it gave me compassion and forced me to practice forgiveness toward myself and others but I had no interest in maintaining that status into my 30's. That's when I started to understand the healing power of a G-D because human means weren't sufficient. That's also when I discovered the need for a program that could address the needs of spiritually minded women who weren't interested in sitting on the mountaintop and refraining from bathing. I could see the need for a system that embraced the sexy mama in all of us, regardless of her stage of becoming. I was so tired of hearing old nasty hags tell me how "un-empowered" I was when they had nothing that I wanted *as I was still young and interested in shaving my armpits.* I ended up in grad school, got into service work in my community and began working as a therapist. Every day that I focus on helping someone else I grow closer to an accurate baseline for functioning. Sure, I'm a bit quirky but I have a level of peace that is altogether stunning thanks to honoring my unique purpose daily. I never thought that I would get married, have kids, have a career and be fulfilled. It was only when I stopped looking outside of myself for a spiritual experience that I realized the answer was there the entire time- within me… That I was enough. That I had always been enough… That I was eternal, forgiven by a benevolent G-D, *capable of forgiving others* and a being **subject to one thing alone… LOVE and my responsibility to pass it along.**

Rita...

In introducing myself to you I want to talk about a quality known as perfectionism. Now, this may sound like a noble quality to have and it may serve most people well, but what do you do when your quest for perfectionism hurts? That is the case with me and what I want to talk to you about ladies. Please don't get so wrapped up in being everything to everyone and having life so perfectly planned, labeled and mapped out that you forget to just "be".

For years I sailed through life as the top achiever. If I did something, I did it better than anybody else.

When I was a kid, I didn't just play baseball, I had to be the "all star". I became my class president, I was a cheerleader, I participated in many sports, activities and then moved into adulthood and didn't have 1 or 2, but 4 children and I did this while juggling a career I excelled at. Any career I have ever wanted to do, I tried it, mastered it and moved on.

I didn't touch drugs and, while I would drink socially, I would never "dream" of becoming an "alcoholic". Isn't that for failures and the weak?

God forbid I ever fail at anything. If I did fail, I just hid my failures and dusted them under the rug as if they never really happened. I was Rita, perfect All-American-Girl from the Midwest. I didn't believe in pre-marital sex, so I justified my "failure in morals" by marrying the dude who I lost my virginity to. We divorced 6 months later after he violently physically attacked me…something I never share with anyone. After all, that information would make people feel "sorry for me" and I don't want their pity.

I didn't allow myself time to mourn and lament things or that might make me have to truly "feel" who I really am! I just maintained Rita the perfect, organized, planned, risk-adverse, gal who nobody really knew.

Perfectionism allowed me to convince myself that I didn't grow up in turmoil and with a lot of trauma, that I never failed and that life really could just be predictable and not scary as shit.

I did all of these things because I had a twisted belief that only "perfect" girls were loved and if I could prove to the world that I was perfect and loveable, then nobody would notice the pain I was suffering at home as a child or then as an adult.

Perfect would keep me protected.

Perfect would keep the nightmares away.

Plastering a smile, raising my kids, doing my job and saving everyone else would make my life worth living.

I was so tightly wound that at some point, I was going to snap!

I wore a mask everyday and pretended to be what I thought everyone else needed me to be. To the outside world, I appeared confident, secure, capable...I was their "go to gal".

Inside, I was hurting, sad, lonely and yet surrounded by people.

I solved everyone else's problems in order to avoid looking at my own. Give me a problem, WHAM! I will find you a solution. I am the girl to run to in a crisis. Why? I have lived through the shit. I have been through the drama. I know all of the games people will play, the next move they will make, how far people will go to hurt another. But, I never shared how I knew this.

When I was younger, I was convinced that all the boys thought I was ugly, all the girls hated me and that I was a big nobody. Lack of self esteem? Hell yes. I was thin, but thought I was chunky. I was pretty and thought I was unattractive. I never thought a boy would like me and yet I always had dates. I was painfully shy and forced myself to be a cheerleader, dancer, student council member, class president, softball player, etc. Anything to prove I wasn't what I knew I was.

I pressed on with my quest for perfectionism as my crutch and my fear of failure is what drove me to never rest or realize who I truly was.

I found myself always on the edge.... I was irritable, cranky, emotionally teetering on this seesaw of falling up and then back down. I was only this way when I was alone, though. I hid this part of me. To everyone else, I was perky, happy Rita.

I could rise to the occasion and then would crash when nobody else was looking. To my friends, I appeared perfect. Inside, I was crumbling. I was an emotional time-bomb waiting to explode and one day I did.

My emotional wake up call.

Prior to that, I lied to myself, I lied to my friends, I lied to my family and I stayed on a path of self destruction rather than just get on a path of finding my true self. Why did I do this to myself? Why didn't I seek out help and find ways to heal my mind and soul so I could have the quality of life I deserved?

.

My quest for perfectionism was how I barely maintained it. My perfectionism hurt. It made me feel like my body was full of mud, nothing flowed. Deep down, I knew I wasn't authentic. I was still this great mother, had a great job, was a good wife and yet things were busted. I was unhappy in my relationship. But I wouldn't let it go. I had to make everything work. I had to fix everything

All of that had to come to an end when I hit rock bottom and I had to get real with myself and admit that I didn't want to go through life with those emotional blinders on anymore. I wanted to take a different approach and make a change and I took the right steps, one day at a time, to do that.

I no longer advocate perfect. Perfect hurts. Perfect is destructive. Perfect is not attainable. Perfect is not the goal.

Being self-actualized is the goal. Now, I insist on knowing myself and I take steps every day to do this. I know my body and my mind and my relationship with myself and my G-D are the driving forces in my life. I will always be on a path of discovering myself. But, today, I am a happy, successful woman who can look in the mirror and say "I love you" and "I know you" and that makes me feel so peaceful. I take each day as an opportunity to become more honest, more open and more satisfied. I have realized that maintaining balance and my relationship with my G-D are the keys to my life.

This realization is why I am a success. You can be a success too in your life if you get real with yourself. I spent years not being authentic. I "thought" I was being authentic and then as I went through the discovery process I realized that who I truly am and who I want to be is NOT what I was portraying to others. Today, my landscape is a peaceful, babbling brook ready to flow on into new experiences. I insist on knowing me. I accept myself bumps, cracks and all. Get open, get real and get authentic. It is the best gift you can give to yourself. The Sexy Mama Manifesto's Guide to Gardening the Soul is my gift to you. I hope you find some inspirational messages to help you get busy becoming.

Coming Home

Any one of us can make the transition from dark to light.

It just takes every bit of energy you've got.

We're here to encourage you to get busy with the doing.

The daily steps and minutia involved with the becoming.

That's why we've been hootin' and hollerin' at you for 200 pages.

We love you so much.

We want you to become the full embodiment of your potential- a living, breathing, forgiving, loving human being.

All that experience of darkness will serve you just as your experience of light has.

This is all great stuff- and is nothing to be feared.

When you encounter evil in the world or dis-ease choose to acknowledge it as someone who is in the process of becoming just as you are.

Choose to see the being as underdeveloped and in dire need of inspiration which is something you are oh so qualified to provide.

You are such a marvelous thing.

So Go On, Girl. Get Busy with Your Becoming… **We need your help!!!**

Glossary of Terms

The Theys: Smart types

The FLL's: Fat, Lazy, Lying Activities

Agency: the ability to make a decision and achieve it successfully, irregardless of social or political constructs.

The Great Woman: a woman who exists for the sole/soul purpose of inspiring others; one who has cut ties with her past and is her own fearless and centered creation. These are the Sexy Mama's matriarchs and sources of inspiration. These are generally older women who are ahead of their time.

Becoming: the activity involved with achieving your dreams

The Sexy Mama: The unique integration of the physical, emotional and spiritual selves. A Great Woman who is manifesting bliss in all areas- personally, vocationally, creatively, spiritually, inspirationally.

Lil Johns/Johnettes: Spawn produced from the Whore and the John
John: the rich dude or poor dude who's buying himself a date with the Whore

Whore: a potentially sexy mama who's too lazy to do the work of evolving and would rather filet herself sexually.

The Chick Filet: the art of systematically reducing your integrity through filleting yourself sexually and/or emotionally.

Fileting: Compromising your integrity sexually and/or emotionally for someone else.

Fat Free: The purposeful path of reducing the fat activities from your life.

Spandex: the scourge of sexy mamas unless you are working out.

Grace Given Talents/ GGT's: qualities that are G-D given.

G-D: the Jewish tradition of referring to a Higher Power as adopted by Sexy Mamas. Describes a force that sustains the Sexy Mama beginning with G and ending with D. Whatever you have in the middle (-) is your business. Can be used interchangeably with the notion of higher self, higher power, or God.

Whoreville: the community wherein whores reside.

The Mysterious Woman: An aspect of the Sexy Mama, can be used interchangeably.

The Self Actualized Woman: An aspect of the Sexy Mama, can be used interchangeably.

Georgia O-Keefe: A 20th century painter who lived in the southwest and painted flowers that upon close examination looked like female reproductive organs. A Great Woman.

Psychic Makeover: When you think you can make your dream man, alchemically, out of a pile of poop using nothing but the powers of manipulation.

DAW's: Discontented American Women

Sacred Muses: Divine Inspiration that encourages individuals along the path of the arts.

Higher Power: something outside of you that you seek for inspiration that is incapable of letting you down; interchangeable with G-D.

The 5 W's and 1 H: Who, What, When Where, Why, How of goal setting.

Spiritual Self: The Soul, Higher Self, Still Small Voice, G-D of the Sexy Mama. Indestructible.

Physical Self: The physical body that exists in this time and place with a distinct set of likes, dislikes and opinions.

Emotional Self: The emotional body that exists in this time and place with a distinct set of likes, dislikes and opinions.

The Ugh Voice: The underdeveloped aspect of the potentially sexy mama that stifles her growth in body and mind through fear of physical and emotional pain, most of which is completely unfounded and non-existent.

Buttinksi: The behind, the rear.

Doc Johnson: vibrator and sexy toy company catering to women.
Groove Thang: rear end, behind.

Sha-bang: excrement, fecal matter.

Uncarved Block: Buddhist terminology meant to describe the highly evolved individual, in the Western Sexy Mama sense we are referring to idiots who've done no work toward evolving and are a bit stupid.

Beast with Two Backs: Shakespeare's word for sex, see Othello.

Society of Gutless Wonders: the fear based congregation of fearful folks.

Stuff: unhealthy storylines, life circumstances that you have no control over, environmental influences that prevent the potentially Sexy Mama from evolving.

Relaxation Script

Read aloud the tasks, recording a copy for yourself.   Observe the tasks in brackets "[]."

Close your eyes.
[take a deep breath]
Smooth your forehead
[take a deep breath]
Unclench your jaw
[take a deep breath]
Allow the cheeks to release
[take a deep breath]
Tilt your chin slightly toward your chest
[take a deep breath]
Release the cords of tension in your neck
[take a deep breath]
Soften your spine
[take a deep breath]
Release your shoulders
[take a deep breath]
Release your sternum
[take a deep breath]
Release your ribs
[take a deep breath]
Release your hips
[take a deep breath]
Release your tailbone
[take a deep breath]
Feel the spine lower deeply into the floor beneath you
[take a deep breath]
Release any resistance in the abdomen by placing your hands on your belly
[take a deep breath]
Feeling the breath rise and fall

[take a deep breath]
Utter a soft sigh that starts out high and dips down low
[take a deep breath]
Utter another sigh as you feel the breath moving lower in the body, from the belly, rather than the chest
[take a deep breath]
Feel the fibers of the legs release and unwind
[take a deep breath]
Feel the upper legs loosen
[take a deep breath]
Feel the knees uncurl
[take a deep breath]
Feel the calves and shins sink more fully into the floor
[take a deep breath]
Feel the ankles and tops of your feet soften
[take a deep breath]
Feel your heels and toes release
[take a deep breath]
Grant yourself permission to sink into the earth
[take a deep breath]
As the body sinks the mind softens
[take a deep breath]
As the body softens the heart widens
[take a deep breath]
As the body sinks the belly moves up and down with the breath
[take a deep breath]
The breath is your cord to the present
[take a deep breath]
The breath will guide you as you continue to sink more fully into the earth
[take a deep breath]
The breath has been there for you from the beginning
[take a deep breath]
Rise and fall with the breath
[take a deep breath]
If a thought should arise

Sexy Mamas Of the Midwest   213
Dallas - Stapleton
Guide To Gardening Your Soul

[take a deep breath]
Let it come as you breathe in and acknowledge it
[take a deep breath]
Let it leave as you breathe out to create more room within
[take a deep breath]
You are limitless
[take a deep breath]
You can accommodate a few funny little thoughts
[take a deep breath]
If they come up
[take a deep breath]
Let them come across the movie screen of your mind's eye as you
breathe in
[take a deep breath]
And fade to black on the picture screen as you breathe out
[take a deep breath]
They are just thoughts
[take a deep breath]
Funny little thoughts
[take a deep breath]
Take this time to acknowledge them
[take a deep breath]
But more importantly take this time to rest
[take a deep breath]
You can pick up all those little cares and concerns when you've
completed your practice… For now, allow those little pictures to fade
to black…
[take a deep breath]
As the thoughts come up witness them
[take a deep breath]
As you breathe out move them out
[take a deep breath]
We are creating more space inside of you through this practice
[take a deep breath]
More neutrality
[take a deep breath]

Sexy Mamas Of the Midwest   214
Dallas - Stapleton
Guide To Gardening Your Soul

You are taking the time to recharge.
[take a deep breath]
You are taking time to know peace of a Higher Power
[take a deep breath]
You are taking time to feel the presence of the space inside of you
[take a deep breath]
Luxuriate in that space inside of you
[take a deep breath]
It is for you and you alone
[take a deep breath]
You can return to this place
[take a deep breath]
This space anytime you need to
[take a deep breath]
Anytime you see fit
[take a deep breath]
This place inside of you is everything becoming
[take a deep breath]
It is your center, your place of new growth
[take a deep breath]
The place where all grace lives
[take a deep breath]
The more you nurture this place inside of you
[take a deep breath]
The more you can return to it more quickly and easily
[take a deep breath]
This is why people meditate
[take a deep breath]
Because you deserve a break
[take a deep breath]
Because you are enough
[take a deep breath]
Just as you are
[take a deep breath]
Right now
[take a deep breath]
Sexy Mamas Of the Midwest   215
Dallas - Stapleton
Guide To Gardening Your Soul

In this moment
[take a deep breath]
You are enough
[take a deep breath]
Because you are so loved
[take a deep breath]
You are so loved
[take a deep breath]
You are so loved

I'm going to let you just rest here for a few moments. Please know that I'm right here beside you the whole time. Looking out for you and keeping you safe. Take this opportunity to let this rest lead you wherever it may. Go ahead and wander...

You're safe!

[End of script]

What Type of Plant Are You?

You are at a party for your boyfriend's office do you...

1.   Not draw a lot of attention to yourself and stay by his side in your role as his girlfriend?

2.   Do I have to go? I am perfectly fine just staying home from this event.

3.   Show what a loving and devoted partner you are and everyone will be naturally drawn to your beauty.

4.   Love being "out" and possibly get a little too rambunctious as the night goes on.

5.   Act charming and open and become everybody's new best friend.

6.   Use the party to make your own connections and pursue your own interests.

7.   Move easily about the room and quickly become the life of the party. Boyfriend who?

8.   Quickly get bored and want to talk him into leaving and do something spontaneous.

9.   Act flirty and friendly and playful.

10.   Look for an interesting group of people to engage with.

11. Use it as an opportunity to make connections for my worthwhile causes.

You are shopping for a wedding dress with your friend and the dress made her look fat AND was too expensive you would…

1. Speak the truth. You get what you get with me. I am always practical

2. Me go shopping for a wedding dress? Forget it! But if I did, I would tell her she looked like hell

3. Guide you gently towards another dress by preserving your feelings. I know how fragile feelings are

4. Let her get the dress if she really wanted it. I am so worried about having friends and afraid of being alone

5. I am very easily wounded by criticism so I would tread lightly and try to move her towards another dress

6. Leave emotion out of it and state the facts. The dress is too tight and you can't afford it. Move on

7. Warmly tell her how beautiful she is and that I think another dress would make her look better

8. Tell her to go with her instincts, if the dress feels right, go for it… but tell her that it doesn't "feel" right to me

9. Have trouble telling her and probably say something silly or funny to distract her

10. Be open and ask her to be open minded and guide her towards something with a little more edge to it

11. Focus on the cost and remind her it is about the marriage and not about the money on a dress

You have been dating a guy for almost 2 months now and he still isn't all that you are looking for so you...

1.   Continue to stay in the relationship to work on it because it is difficult for you to break the rules and leave.

2.   I've been in a relationship that long? If it isn't going well, I leave. I know that something will come along.

3.   Push too hard to make the relationship perfect and ignore your intuition.

4.   Stay in the relationship because you feel unfilled without a partner.

5.   End the relationship but get really resentful and spiteful if he moves on.

6.   Use the facts as evidence and determine the relationship should end.

7.   Leave the relationship quickly if you are not feeling valued or loved.

8.   Will continue to strive for harmony because you are in love with being in love with him.

9.   Move on, I'm bored with this guy.

10. Let go and find someone else. If I don't feel it by now, I will never feel it.

11. I have to let go and focus on my true callings in life and not waste time on this anymore.

Which of the following best describes you…

1.   I will date one person at a time for a long period of time

2.   I need a partner who lets me have my freedom

3.   I can be very high maintenance. I require great care and nuturing, but I give it back ten-fold

4.   I will often put relationships before my own personal needs

5.   I am a romantic and love flowers, poetry and candelit dinners

6.   I will often remain friends after a relationship ends

7.   I am generous to a fault and I write poems, give cards and other tokens of love

8.   I am very in tune with my body and my sensuous side

9.   I like a lot of attention in a relationship and am very playful and rarely depressed or down

10. I like to dominate my relationships. Wimps, need not apply

11. My relationships come second to my "causes"

Your thoughts on the "L" word

1.   I am practical about love and value traditional roles in relationships

2.   I don't enjoy talking about feelings and love

3.   I have an ideal standard of what love is

4.   I have a fear that people will reject my love

5.   Love is the ideal feeling. I'm a romantic

6.   It is what it is. Emotions are left out of it

7.   The more "touchy feely" the better

8.   I am in love with love

9.   Love is a flirty, fun feeling

10. When I fall in love, I fall hard. But it is difficult for me to fall in love

11. True love comes from within

When it comes to my career the following statement best applies…

1. I will rise to positions of responsibility in any career or organization that I am part of

2. I am drawn to careers that are structured, independent and allow me to tap into my practical, logical side

3. I am a mother or teacher as I provide inspiration to children

4. I am drawn to careers in performance, sales or that put me in the "limelight"

5. I am happiest in careers that are people driven and service-oriented

6. I like careers that allow me to be an active, independent problem-solver

7. I am drawn to careers where I can be of direct service to people

8. I need a career where I can remain flexible and adaptable while working with people

9. I need an adaptable, flexible schedule. I get bored easily

10. I am drawn to the creative arts, photography, writing

11. I am happiest when I am giving back to the community

How would your friends describe you?

1.   I'm a traditional girl and I make a good friend because I am reliable and stable

2.   Will rise to meet the needs of most occasions, and is serious and reserved

3.   I value friendships, am a good listener and a devoted partner

4.   I love to meet the needs of others and love to be around other people

5.   I am everyone's friend, always on the go, the ultimate PTA/soccer mom

6.   I am laid back and I go with the flow. I am not a social butter fly

7.   I am enthusiastic about everything, friendly and warm. I am the life of the party

8.   I am compassionate and easy going. Very modest and deep

9.   I don't like to sit still. Punctuality is not my thing. People love to be around me

10. Mysterious, intellectual and open-minded. My clothing may confuse them sometimes

11. Eco friendly, strong views and well-read. Doesn't wasted time on material things. Loyal to close friends

How would you describe yourself?

1.   I'm a private person. I prefer familiar friends to making new ones. I will typically follow the rules

2.   I enjoy solitude. I am athletic and healthy. I have a difficult time with long term commitments. I am logical

3.   I am very empathetic. I can be hurt easily. I am as warm as I am complex. I value my friendships

4.   Being out is more comfortable than being alone. I am clever and warm. I fear rejection.

5.   My life is an open door policy. I love to join clubs/activities. I am easily wounded by criticism.

6.   I am flexible and all about action. I pursue my own activities first. I don't say my feelings, I show them.

7.   It is better to give than to receive. I want to be appreciated. I am always upbeat. I have a ton of friends

8.   I am sensuous and drink in life. I am well rounded and easy going. I am on the cutting edge

9.   Playful, fun and I act ditzy although I am not. I am unpredictable and I hate to sit still. I am rarely "down"

10.   I am edgy and a bit sassy. I will always try new things. I am eclectic and know how to push the boundaries

11.   I am generous with my resources. Sensitive and health conscience. A Strong sense of self worth.

Congratulations! You're finished! Add up all of your numbers before the item that best describes you and go to the Plant Index on the following pages for your description.

The Plant Index

Marigold

0 – 8

A Marigold is all about order and structure.

She is private – She doesn't like a lot of attention and she will not draw a lot of attention to herself

She is reliable, stable and consistent in all that she does – work, play, friendships

She prefers familiar friends to making new ones

A marigold is Down-to-earth and enjoys peaceful living

She will typically follow the rules due to her sense of reason and logic

She can be counted on to be appropriate

A marigold will date one person at a time for a long period of time.

A marigold wants to mate for life as that is what the rules say you should do

She may stay in a bad relationship because it is too hard to break the rules and leave

She is practical and realistic

She has a dry, intellectual sense of humor

She is a traditional girl and values traditional roles

She makes a great friend to keep your grounded. She makes good decisions based on reason

You get what you get with a marigold

She will rise to positions of responsibility in any career or organization she is part of

The Plant Index

Tulip

9 – 16

Tulips don't require a lot of physical affection

She is logical and practical

She is extremely self-sufficient and requires little or no nurturing

This girl is serious, dutiful and reserved

She is perfectly ok being alone for long periods of time – enjoys solitude and stands on her own

She is more comfortable with impersonal dealings rather than deep connections at times

Tulips need partners who respect personal freedom

She may work long stretches before coming up for air

She can withstand great relationship droughts because she knows the rain will eventually come

She will rise to meet the needs of most occasions

She isn't going to talk about her feelings with her partner. The relationship speaks for itself

She is athletic, healthy and pursues interests with intensity

She has a difficult time with long-term commitments

She is drawn to careers that are structured, independent allow her to tap her practical, logical side.

The Plant Index

Rose

17 – 24

Every rose has its thorns – There are 2 sides to the rose and she tries to hide them both

People are naturally drawn to her because they sense her loving nature

She has no idea how beautiful she is

She values friendships but puts them behind family and faith

She has an ideal standard of what love is or what a relationship should be

Her outer beauty is natural. Her mind is complex

She is very empathetic to the cause of others

She is as warm as she is complex

Her strong intuition helps her know good from evil

This girl is a perfectionist and she will bring out her thorns if you get in the way

She is very fragile – you can hurt her easily

She is full of integrity and makes decisions based on her values

She will be a good listener and a devoted partner

She may push too hard to make the relationship perfect

She can be high maintenance. Requires great care but will give it back ten-fold

She makes an excellent mother or teacher as she is warm, patient and inspirational to her children

The Plant Index

25 – 32

Pussy Willow

She loves to meet other people's needs

She prefers to surround herself with others

She is rambunctious

She often feels pulled between physical needs and spiritual gain

The Pussy Willow enjoys meditation and journaling as a way to express her true self

She will put relationships before personal needs

She sometimes feels unfulfilled without a partner

Being "out" is more comfortable to her than being home alone

She has an intense fear of rejection

She is smooth, clever and warm

She makes decisions based on her past experiences

She is not deeply interested in scholastic pursuits and instead prefers real world knowledge

She is drawn to careers in performance, sales or those that put her in the limelight

33 – 40

Buttercup

Her life is an open-door policy – she is everyone's best friend

She is intense, personable and warm

She's an idealist. Always moving onto the next thing, convinced it will be perfect and successful

Buttercup is cute rather than beautiful so nobody is threatened by her

She is very talkative and open

She will be in many clubs, activities and is on the go. She is the ultimate PTA mom.

They make responsible partners.

She is very easily wounded by criticism and has difficulty taking feedback

She can get resentful and spiteful if you piss her off

She expects flowers, poetry, candlelit dinners. Remember, she is an idealist, so love is always ideal.

People turn to her for nuturing and support. They make natural mothers

She is so charming and even tempered that a man could easily victimize her

She is drawn to careers that are people driven and service-oriented

The Plant Index

41 – 48

Daylily

A Daylily is your practical girl

She is realistic, flexible and action oriented

She prefers to have a few close friends who have similar interests

She is not your social butterfly. She likes her activities or her solitude

She is really laid-back and goes with the flow

She will always have time to pursue her own interests

She may ignore personal relationships as she focuses on herself

She thinks she can get things done more effectively on her own and prefers it

This girl is a realist when it comes to love. It is what it is.

She would rather demonstrate her feelings than say them

She will use "facts" and evidence to determine if a relationship should end. Emotions are left out.

A Daylily will remain friends after the relationship

She doesn't "get" perfectionists and she is tolerable of disorder

Her ties to people tend to be more superficial

She likes careers that allow her to be an active, independent problem solver

The Plant Index

Holly

49 – 56

Holly is friendly, warm and outgoing

Her philosophy is it is better to give than to receive

She is bold and refreshing and is the life of the party

She is enthusiastic about everything she does and the world she lives in

She is conscience of the environment and gives back to the earth

Holly is usually very popular and have lots of friends

She wants to be appreciated

She will leave relationships quickly if they get too stagnant or she doesn't feel valued

She is very "touchy-feely" and will write poems, give cards, gifts and tokens of love

She moves on very quickly when a relationship ends

A Holly is witty and upbeat and she loves a good party

She is generous to a fault

She will pretend that everything in her life is "ok" and put up a good front

She has a strong intuitive side and can read people quickly

She needs a partner who enjoys her giving nature

She wants a career where she can be with people and be of direct service to others

Lilac

57 – 64

She is compassionate, quiet and elegant

She is very modest and is unaware of her own beauty

She is very in tune with her body and her sensuous side

She drinks in life and is in touch with nature and the senses

Her emotions are well-rounded and she has a strong sense of "being"

Many are drawn to her but she chooses friends who share her similar values

She is easy going and amendable until her principles are challenged

Everything she does is with depth and meaning

She is rarely judgemental and is openly accepting of many

She is a strong advocate for victims and understands their plights

The lilac is in love with being in love

She may abandon all she has for simple pleasures

Lilacs nourish their relationships and strive for harmony

She is trendy and will be on the cutting edge

She can be impulsive and spontaneous

Bougainvillea

65 – 72

She is playful, silly and quite disorganized

She can sometimes act a little "ditzy" but people love to be around her

Friends should expect her to show up on time as punctuality is not her thing

This is the girl who will agree to help you move, but be careful that she actually shows up

It is hard for her to be depressed or "down"

Bougainvillea are unpredictable

She is very flirty and friendly

They have a tendency to be smothering in a relationship if they aren't getting enough attention

She can be serious and intellectual when needed but would rather roll out the fun and let loose

Sometimes she feels the need to be the center of attention

She doesn't like to sit and listen… she likes to move and do

She gets bored easily so relationships are a struggle for her

She prefers a career that is adaptable where she can have a flexible schedule

The Plant Index

Petunia

72 – 80

This girl is very mysterious and seductive

She is adventurous and enjoys taking risks

She is a rocker at heart.

She is open-minded and will try new things

She is edgy, sassy and is usually very intellectual

Petunia dominates most of her relationships and the men prefer it that way

When she falls for a man, she falls hard, but it takes a lot to win her heart.

Her friendships are as eclectic as she is, artists, doctors, teachers, mothers, engineers, you name it.

She is good at hiding emotions

She recharges her batteries by reading, painting or doing something solo

Petunia knows how to push the boundaries and not worry about the consequences

Sometimes what she wears may confuse other people but it suits mood

She has a way of viewing the world that makes other want to be around her
She prefers careers in the creative arts

The Plant Index

81 – 88

Daisy is generous with all of her resources
She has strong views and appears flexible until challenged
She is very health conscience and may be a vegetarian
She gives back to the earth and is very eco friendly and takes on many causes
She has strong philosophical views and is very well-read
Her relationships come second to her "causes" and her "victims"
Daisy doesn't allow her sensitivity to get in the way of her decisions
She has many pets and finds comfort in their company
She doesn't waste her time on material things or monetary gains
She has a deep sense of self worth
She has found her true calling in life and knows her G-D
Her close friends know that she is loyal to the end
She is vulnerable to break ups because she forgets to put time into her relationships
She is happiest in careers where she gives back to the community